LIVING WITH BUBBA

The Ballad of Bubba Ledbetter

COMING SOON

The Soul Seekers — This book will make you wonder about what you eat on Halloween. Some candies are not meant to be eaten, but destroyed.

The Legend of Hell's Gate — When a book writer takes a trip to an old cemetery to work on a book, the cemetery takes charge and the cemetery becomes the book.

Graveside Manners — Someone opened the seal that should never have been opened. Someone let the hidden things out that should have never been freed. Someone will pay with their life. Someone did this without graveside manners.

Living with Bubba: The Redneck Life — This is the second part to the brainy comedy of Bubba and his life. The laughter continues as Bubba and his family tries out new ways of doing things in life. If you liked part one of Living with Bubba, this will make you laugh twice as hard.

Author Website

www.pcbeachbumnews.com

LIVING WITH BUBBA

The Ballad of Bubba Ledbetter

A White Knight Original

(White Knight is a trademark of Daniel Reeves)

Daniel M. Reeves

Published by Lulu, Inc.

Morrisville, NC

ISBN 978-1-4303-0652-8

For Patricia,

Happiness is all that we make in this world. We are the craftsmen of our own dreams. I have had a wonderful life with you and I am thankful that we crafted our life together many years ago.

Love Daniel

Preface

Living with Bubba is a book about the perils of Bubba Ledbetter and his family. This book will take you on a redneck journey that will keep you laughing all the way there. The story starts out with how the family came to be, and then it carries you to the life that Bubba accidentally fell into.

Living with Bubba is a unique glance at how time forgot one man and catching up with the rest of the world is an adventure that will leave the reader laughing hysterically. Grab a soda and some snacks, and then sit back and enjoy the story.

Chapter One

Bubba's Father

Now before there was Bubba Ledbetter, there was Jed Ledbetter, his father. Jed was raised by his sisters and they did not teach him too much of anything. He learned most of everything he knew by experience and experience for him normally meant that somebody was going to lose something. He had several jobs, but by the end of the day what he did not destroy, could never be fixed. Most of the people in the community would not open the door when they seen him coming. They felt sorry for him, but not sorry enough to let him in.

One time he was given a job for a logging company. He had lied to the owner to get the job. He told the owner that he could cut more trees than they had ever seen. The boss was convinced that Jed could cut trees so he agreed to give him the job. "Go get your chainsaw and start cutting these trees into six feet pieces. I will come back and check on you late this evening," the boss informed Jed. Now Jed never owned a chainsaw in his life, nor had never seen one.

Jed knew that for him to have this job he would need him one of those chainsaws. He made his way to town and went into the local hardware store. Now Jed had no money, but to get rid of him before the store burnt down the owner decided to extend Jed some credit. Jed was excited. He felt that the world was beginning to smile on him. The store owner felt somehow sorry for Jed and decided to gas the saw up for Jed after which Jed thanked him for everything and left the store without incident.

Jed had been gone for about six hours when the store owner heard the door open and Jed walked in. The sight was one to behold. Jed was soaking wet from sweat and he looked like he had been whipped. The store owner met Jed and asked, "Did that saw do the trick, Jed?"

There was no answer that came from Jed. He sat right down in the middle of the floor. "You ok, Jed?" the store owner asked. "Yea, ima kind of tired. This chainsaw is not too good. I barely cut up one tree all day long," Jed explained.

The store owner moved the chainsaw to the middle of the floor so he could take a look and see what was wrong with the saw. He pulled on the rope and the saw fired right up. He raced it up a few times and Jed looked really puzzled. He tapped the store owner on the shoulder and asked, "What did you do to make that chainsaw make a noise. It never made any kind of noise like that when I was pushing it back and forth on that tree?" The store owner could not believe that Jed had worked all day cutting up a tree with the saw and never realized that he needed to crank the thing.

Now the story is not about Jed Ledbetter, but you will need the information about Jed to be able to understand why Bubba is Bubba. It seemed to be a family thing and Jed's parents did not make it to see the outcome of Jed. Some say they accidentally fell off of a bridge one day, but others say that after they realized how Jed Ledbetter was, they killed themselves to find peace. Of course it was very difficult for the sheriff not to believe suicide due to the fact that each accidentally fell at the same time from different locations on the bridge.

Now the five sisters blamed it all on Jed because they said that he was too dumb for anyone to teach. The girls had tried, but everything they told Jed to do he would get it backwards and something would get broken. All of the girls had seen the local doctor at some point in time during the attempted teaching of Jed. They finally gave him the job of slopping the hogs. However, the problem with that job came when it was time for the hogs to go to the market. Jed came up with his own idea that he should pretend he was slopping hogs until they got new ones to slop.

Every day Jed would get up and go out where the hogs used to be. He would make certain that there was plenty of water and feed put out for the hogs that weren't there. The girls did not mind how stupid he looked, but it was getting expensive and the feed was pilling up. They decided to make certain that when they sold the hogs, they bought some baby piglets before they returned home from the market. They figured that would keep Jed busy and not cost any extra money.

The girls had always lived a reclusive life without many of the necessities that go along with it. They had no indoor plumbing or electricity and the only transportation they had was a horse and wagon. Jed walked everywhere he went. No one had ever taught him how to drive an automobile or the horse drawn wagon for that matter. He had really never seen an automobile up close. He was afraid of them.

Before his parents died, he was in the front yard playing with an old pole that he found. He suddenly heard a strange noise coming down the old dirt road. It sounded to him like thunder roaring. Within a moment, something came into his view. It was a motorcycle and Jed had never seen one before. He thought it was some kind of a monster and it had grabbed a man. Jed used the pole that he was playing with and knocked the man right off the back of the motorcycle, breaking his arm, leg, and a few ribs. Of course that was another reason people believed his parents committed suicide.

Now at first, Jed liked being around people. He liked to look at girls and wanted them to look at him, but that was never going to happen for him. While he was in town he seen many people going into a bowling alley. He had no idea what the place was, but he decided to go in and see. He noticed how people were throwing the big rocks down the isles and how they would knock over the things at the end of the isle. He was amazed at the game they were playing. His only problem was that he felt he could not afford one of those rocks they were using. He decided that maybe he could make his own playing rock.

Jed looked for days, trying to find a perfectly round rock. Finally, he came up with one that was close. It was not perfectly round, but he could get it to roll. Jed had remembered how those rocks the people were using at the place had three holes in the top. He found an old chisel that had belonged to his father and chiseled out three holes in the rock. He had also found some red paint in the barn so he decided that it would be a good idea if he painted his rock, just like everybody else's.

When Jed entered the bowling alley no one noticed that he had a giant rock instead of a ball. He walked up to one of those lanes like he was a professional. He looked around to see if any of the girls were looking at him. He wanted them to see him on his début with bowling. No one was paying any attention to him and he figured that if he started playing they would. "Watch this," he screamed as he drew back the rock and threw it hard down one of the lanes.

The rock was so heavy that not only did it bust all of the pins into little pieces, but it also knocked several big holes in the lane. Everybody was watching at that point. He figured he had gotten it right and everybody was watching him because he was so good. His rock came back on the return and he decided to try another lane. He drew back again and this time let the rock go as hard as it could. Of course there were several things broken when the rock hit the end of the alley. He turned around and smiled big for everyone. Unfortunately, the owner of the bowling alley did not see him to be a winner and threw him out. He was to never return.

Jed had been to church a few times, but he was not very fond of going. The preacher seemed to scare him talking so much about dying and going to a place called hell. His sisters had not been very assuring with church for Jed either. Whenever Jed would go to church his sisters would convince him that the preacher had actually preached the sermon on something that was going to happen to Jed. There was one sermon that the preacher had preached about Adam and Eve. The preacher had spoke of how god had created the woman and how Adam had been put into a deep sleep so the woman could be made.

Now Jed was a deep sleeper anyhow. The girls had created a plan and Jed was the target. One evening Jed had fallen asleep on the floor. The sisters gathered around Jed and pinched him real hard on his side. Jed suddenly awoke and noticed that the sisters were all around him. "What's going on. My side's a hurting real bad?" Jed asked. He was puzzled about his sisters. They looked at him real seriously and said, "Jed, you're having a wife."

Of course, Jed took that very seriously. He knew that his side was hurting and he remembered how god put Adam in a deep sleep. His sisters convinced him that he would have to stay in bed until the wife was born. He had stayed in bed for almost two weeks before he decided that the wife would have to be born with him up and walking about.

That was not the worst thing that the girls had done to Jed. A County Fair had come to town and Jed had never been to one. The girls had planned on Jed's demise. Jed was slopping the hogs and the girls came out to where he was. They informed him that a big thing had come to town and there were some smaller horses that he could learn how to ride. Jed had wanted to learn to ride a horse, but was too afraid of the large horse they had. The girls informed Jed that they would go into town that night and let him learn how to ride. He was pleased.

Jed and the sisters had made it to town and Jed was amazed at the sight of everything. The sisters led him to the horses and made him get on. "Something is wrong with these horses and they scare me," Jed informed his sisters. They assured him that everything would be fine if he would just get on one of the horses. After much coaxing, he finally climbed on.

After only a short moment the horse sprang into action. It galloped along at a steady pace, but Jed had begun to slip from the saddle in terror. He grabbed for the horses mane, but could not get a firm grip. He tried his best to throw his arms around the horse's neck, but he slid down the side of the horse anyhow. "Help me, Ima falling!" Jed screamed.

Jed finally decided to throw himself away from the horse and try not to get trampled. Unfortunately, his foot became entangled in the stirrup and he was at the mercy of the horse's pounding hooves as his head struck the ground again and again. He felt like he was doomed and would go unconscious at any time. Suddenly, one of the workers at the fair noticed what was happening and made a dash to help Jed. The worker grabbed the power cord that powered the merry-go-round and unplugged the sucker. Jed would survive, but the sisters were merciless with their laughter of him and the toy horse.

Chapter Two

Before Bubba Was Born

During the summer of 1954, the Ledbetter sisters and Jed had put on their best dress clothes, which were not very much at all, and went to the local church. It had been a few weeks since Jed had seen the inside of a church and he was curious about what the man with the shotgun was doing with the boy at the front of the church. It seems that one of the local boys and girls had met with love and the father had met them both with a shotgun.

Jed was seventeen and still knew nothing about girls or marriage. He noticed a boy that was close to the same age as he. Dale Clemens had a bad reputation of getting people into a lot of trouble. Jed was too curious about what was happening at the front of the church and curiosity was just about to kill the cat. Jed turned to Dale Clemens for his answer.

"What them folks a doing up there?' Jed asked. Dale looked real sneaky. Jed might as well been asking a snake if it would give him a kiss on his cheek. Dale set his eyes on Jed and spoke in a real low tone so no one would be able to hear what he was telling Jed.

"You Jed Ledbetter, aint ye? That shotgun is a gift for the boy up front and they are also gonna give him that pretty woman to do as he pleases with. She'll have to cook and clean everyday for that boy," Dale said. Now Jed was interested in hearing that. He could hardly believe his ears that the boy was going to get him a new gun and a woman that would slave after him.

Jed had never been out on a date and didn't know the first thing there was to know about women. He had no clue as to what he could say to a girl to get her to agree with such an arrangement as being given to him.

Somehow Jed was about to find out the exact way to do that. Growing up around girls, Jed never knew that some guys liked playing pranks on other guys. He had no idea that things like that went on.

Jed moved closer to Dale and whispered, "How do you think I can get me a woman and a new gun like that boy's a getting up front there? He's a real lucky one and I want to get just exactly what he's a getting. Tell me what I got a do," Jed said. Dale grinned widely.

Dale knew that by now Jed looked a lot like bait. "Well here's what ye got a do. First, you have to find you a woman. I think that Virginia gal behind us will do just fine for you. Go tell her you need to show her something and get her to go to the barn out back. When you get in the barn, take off all yer clothes and holler "Somebody help us. We in here a lovin. Now don't you forget that you gotta keep hollerin until somebody hears. You will surely get to see that new gun today," Dale said. "Well I'll be a dog. It's that easy," Jed said. Dale looked sneaky again. "It is that easy, Jed and I are with you all the way," Dale explained.

Dale moved away from Jed and watched him out the side of his eye. Dale only hoped that Jed Ledbetter was as stupid as he had heard from everyone around the community. Dale knew that if he pulled this off, Jed would surely be in the biggest pot of hot water before the day was through.

Jed was shy about girls, but he sure did want one of those new guns that the boy up front was getting. Jed looked back at Virginia and she at first tried to ignore him. Too late, she made eye contact with Jed Ledbetter. She was only sixteen, but deep down inside she had much more sense than Jed. On this day she had left them at home.

"Hey. I've gotta show you something important out back. It's a frog with three heads and you just gotta see it. It's amazing," Jed said, and then he moved from the church pew into the isle. Virginia was curious about a three-headed frog. She had never seen such a thing and curiosity would kill her if she did not go and see. She eased herself out of the pew and followed Jed outside. Jed kept looking back to make certain that Virginia girl was following him to her doom.

Now Virginia's father did not believe in jokes of any kind. He was a strict man and he believed that a woman and a man together in any form spelled wedlock. He was busy up at the front of the church, but he did see his youngest daughter slip out.

Jed and Virginia had made their way to the big barn at the back of the church. Jed opened the door and the both of them walked into the barn. "Where's the funny frog?" she asked. Jed said, "Ima fixing to show you." Jed pulled off all of his clothes and Virginia was shocked. She was angry and pushed him backward against the door. He started yelling, "Wahoo. Somebody help us. We in here a lovin!"

Suddenly, the door pushed swiftly open and knocked Jed on top of Virginia. She was fit to be tied, but her father, Wade Haney, could not have been any madder at seeing his daughter with Jed. Jed had noticed Wade out of the corner of his eye. He gave wade a big smile and said, "Give me my new gun and woman. I know I've earned them."

Virginia's father made an angry face and spit some tobacco juice out the side of his mouth. "Your shotgun's right here," her father said, then fired a load of buckshot into Jed's butt. Jed was screaming something awful as if he had been attacked by a colony of hornets. Jed had never felt such pain in his life.

The entire church had made their way outside when they heard the gunshot and commotion. The ceremony had stopped and even the preacher was looking on at what was happening. Jed was rolling around on the ground and he was rubbing his naked and bleeding butt all over the ground. The sisters were astonished, but thought that the entire thing was funny. They had only dreamed of seeing Jed in such a predicament as what he had gotten himself in on this day.

The preacher dragged Jed into the church and started digging the buck shot out of Jed's butt. At the same time Wade was explaining the ins and outs of marriage to his soon to be son-in-law. Jed insisted that everything was just a big mistake and that he didn't even know what to do with a wife. After Virginia's father explained in vivid detail what having his new wife meant, Jed was crying like a baby. He had not been aware that a regular job was included in the woman/gun package deal.

One of Jed's sisters felt that it was time to take advantage of the situation. She whispered into Jed's ear and told him that if he was in a barn alone with a girl, then that meant he was supposed to marry her. Jed was confused. He had never been told that before. Of course he knew that he had never been told a lot of things before, so he believed his sister. The shotgun wedding that was supposed to have been for just one of Wades' daughters ended up being for two.

Wade Haney did give the newlyweds an old house with some livestock. Being that the old house was farther from town than where Jed had lived, walking would be a problem. Wade Haney gave Jed an old crazy mule that he could use to ride to town. Jed had to begin his own farm and he always felt like he had missed out on his real life calling, to which Jed had no clue as to what it was. However, the sisters were ecstatic that Jed would no longer be around to cause them more problems. They felt maybe it would be possible for them to find spouses now.

Virginia never forgave Jed for what he had done to the both of them. She had liked a couple of other guys that she was in school with. Lee was her favorite boyfriend, but Roy also had a place in her heart. She had thought that someday she would end up married to one of those boys.

She had never paid any attention to Jed in her life. He had never been a thought as far as anything went. He was stupid and she felt that he probably was the worst person on the face of the planet. Of course her planet was small. She too had been basically isolated from the rest of the world. Her father kept a very short leash on her. She was not allowed to go anywhere alone, or do anything without one of the parents being present.

The Haney family believed in the old way. They also did not have inside plumbing or electricity. Wade felt that luxury items were evil and would cause the soul to perish if the pleasures became too great. He worked form daylight to dark, six days a week. He felt it his duty to keep his daughters in a safe environment. Somehow that safety net vanished and he was devastated knowing that he had failed.

The old house Wade gave to Virginia and Jed was a dump. When Jed first went to see it he could not because the grass was so high. He walked all the way back to Wade Haney's house just to get new directions. Virginia's mother finally convinced Virginia that it was the right thing to do and not to be mad at Jed. Virginia decided that she would take Jed to the new house and let him see what was in store for him. She figured that maybe that would be some revenge for what he had done to her. She could not wait to see the look on his face when he seen the house. She could not wait to see his expression when he realized how much work he was in for.

After the visit, Jed ran back home to his sisters. He was crying like a big baby. The big problem he found was that the sisters would not let him in. They would not even come to the door. They pretended to be gone, but Jed knew they were there. He had seen them looking out the window behind the curtain. Jed reluctantly went back and waded through the tall grass to the place that he would forever call home.

After Wade Haney finally realized that he had gave his daughter away to an idiot, he finally took the responsibility in helping them fix up the house and move in. Jed had no idea about how to do carpentry work. That is why Wade Haney did all of the work and Jed mainly watched. The house looked good when Wade finally finished the last coat of paint. However, Jed looked much like the house because every time he turned around, he was leaning against the freshly painted house.

Jed spent much of his time trying to learn how to ride the old mule. He had fallen off so many times that Wade Haney became accustomed to hearing the big thump. At first Wade would stop working on the house long enough to check and see if Jed was alright. Finally, Wade realized that if Jed got killed trying to learn to ride the mule, his daughter would be a widow and for him that might be fine. Unfortunately for Wade, that never happened because Jed always managed to land on something that was not hard. He eventually learned to stay on the mule.

After the house was completed, Virginia's mother had gathered up some dishes and bed clothes that she felt Jed and Virginia would be able to use. Jed and Virginia spent the first few days and nights in the house, trying to figure out what it was they were supposed to do. They knew that marriage meant something, but they had not yet figured that part out.

Virginia Ledbetter was not stupid by any means. She was just deprived of knowing certain things that now might be important to know. Wade Haney figured that those certain tidbits of information would come to his kids by nature. Unfortunately, those things did not come and Virginia was in the same shoes as Jed was on certain tidbits of important information.

One of the houses in the neighborhood had stood empty for a couple of years. The Miller couple had lived a very long life and both had passed away during the same year. The house was left to the son, Terry Miller, and he had taken all that he wanted from the house. He had heard about Jed's marriage to Virginia and about them moving into the old Wade house. He knew they would need some furnishings and things for the house. Terry stopped by and informed Jed that if he would clean out the old house, he could have anything that he found. Jed agreed and the deal was set.

While Jed was cleaning out the house he stumbled upon something that took him by surprise. He had stumbled upon a ladies hand-held mirror. Jed had never seen a mirror before in his life. Now while his sisters had seen a mirror, they never allowed Jed into their rooms and his knowledge was small on such girly things. Virginia had never seen one either. Her father would not allow one in the house and no one had informed her that such an item existed.

Jed first looked at the back of the mirror. It was all silver looking and felt cool to the touch. When he turned the mirror over and looked deeply into the mirror he was amazed. "Why that looks just like me daddy. I just a wonder why these Miller folk had a picture of my daddy," Jed thought to himself.

He was amazed at how the eyes seemed to follow his every move and each time he would smile at the photo, the photo seemed to smile right back. Jed placed his ear next to the mirror and said, "Daddy is that really you? I can see you making those faces at me, but I just can't her nothing". There was no answer and Jed just thought that it was because his daddy was dead and all.

Later that evening, Jed was interested in finding out if Virginia knew about the moving pictures. Jed never got into an appropriate name to call Virginia so he just called her girl. Jed walked up to her while she was working on getting a curtain in the living room hung. "Girl, have you ever seen a moving picture?" Jed asked her. She was standing on a chair and she turned and looked down at Jed.

"No I have not, but the last time that you asked me if I ever saw anything, I ended up in a real big mess. I don't think that I want to see anything that you got," she informed Jed. He stepped back a couple of feet, turned and walked away. He was not mad at her or anything. He just figured that she had her likes and ideas and he had his. He would just keep the moving picture a secret from Virginia.

Every day Jed would slip out to the barn a few times and take a look at the moving photo of his father. Virginia became suspicious of Jed slipping out. She was not good at living with curiosity. She did not like surprises and she did not like secrets being kept from her, no matter who was keeping the secret. That is why she ended up in the predicament she was in with Jed.

Now women make good spies and Virginia was not going to allow some secret between her and the man she had to marry. She knew that Jed had something out in the barn and she was determined to find out what exactly it was that Jed was hiding from her. She knew that she also did not want Jed to know that she was too curious about his life and the secret things he kept in it. She would have to secretly find out and not let Jed know that she did.

One day she waited for Jed to go off to town and she went to the barn. She searched that barn inside out. She looked under things and all on top of everything and she was searching for something that was suspicious. There was a board near the bottom of the wall and it was loose. She found a shovel and was able to pry the board the rest of the way up. She was desperate to find the item before Jed returned.

There, just inside the wall was the secret. Virginia was fit to be tied. She had never been so mad in all of her life and Jed was going to get it when he came home. She looked close at the picture and the picture seemed to follow her every move. It seemed to almost be alive and yet she was angry, she was also amazed at what the item was. She thought that the girl in the photo was pretty and that it could have been even prettier than she.

Jed had ruined her life and now he had him a girlfriend she thought. She was furious. She looked deeper at the photo and noticed that the picture must have been taken right there in the barn. She wondered how Jed could do that to her. She wondered how he could slip some girl in the barn and use a fancy camera to take some strange girl's picture. He had never been interested in taking her picture, she thought.

Virginia was so mad that she stuck her tongue out at the girl in the picture. At the same time, the girl in the picture stuck her tongue out at Virginia. She became even madder at Jed and the girl in the picture. Only Jed was not there for her to take out vengeance on. She threw the picture down, and then picked it back up and looked at the girl. "You stupid bitch. If you will come out of that picture, I'll beat your butt," Virginia screamed into the mirror. The girl in the mirror did not answer back. Virginia walked out of the barn with the mirror.

That evening she was waiting for Jed on the porch swing of the house. He was riding up the road on the old mule, toward the old house, like he was a king. He rode into the yard and stepped down from the mule. Virginia got up from the swing and met him. She had the old mirror in her hand and she was mad. "Who the hell is this bitch in the photo that keeps making bad faces at me, and what are you doing with it?" she questioned as she gave Jed the mirror. Jed looked puzzled. "That is no bitch you are talking about. Why that's my dead daddy!" Jed screamed. "You liar. That is a photo of your new girlfriend," Virginia argued back. They fussed for hours swapping the mirror back and forth.

Jed would look at the mirror and smile because his dead father would smile back at him. It would make Virginia that much more madder at Jed, thinking that he was smiling at the girl. She would grab the mirror from him and cuss the girl again that was in the mirror. Jed would grab it back and admire what he was seeing in the mirror.

Now the house was not that far away from other houses and the noise had brought out some of the neighbors. Most of the neighbors knew of Virginia and Jed, but did their best to stay away. One of the neighbors finally came over to see what all of the ruckus was about. When she realized that Jed and Virginia had been arguing over a mirror, she was consumed in laughter, which did not set too well with Virginia or Jed.

After the neighbor had collected herself from the moment of intense comedy, she sat them both down and explained what the mirror was. She had to actually make both of them look in the mirror at the same time for them to see that the faces change from person to person. They were amazed. Jed had never seen his reflection and did not know that he looked like his father. Virginia had also never seen her reflection and did not realize how beautiful she was. The neighbor felt really sorry for the couple. She could not believe that the two had never seen a mirror. She also wondered what else the two unfortunate kids did not know.

For the rest of the day and all of the night, Jed and Virginia shared the mirror. Both wanted to see their reflection and they spent hours on end looking in the mirror and laughing. That night they became friends as they shared the new experience of the mirror. One would even think that maybe they even fell in love.

Chapter Three

The Misunderstanding

A year had passed since Jed and Virginia were married. Jed had learned many things from Wade Haney and had become quiet the farmer. Jed and Virginia had become real close and their relationship had begun to develop. They talked about everything and sometimes they would talk the night through. They had become happy with their new life together. They believed that the closeness they shared was something that had been missing all of their lives.

Jed and Virginia were still new to the married life and did not know many things about how it all worked. Now Jed and Virginia were not aware that married couples slept together and the two did not share the same bedroom at night. Jed had his and Virginia had hers. Nonetheless, the two hardly spent the night in their bedrooms as they would usually talk all night.

Wade Haney owned a logging company and knew that Jed was not good at much of anything. He wanted to give Jed a job so he could support his daughter, but he was afraid to give Jed just any job. Wade knew that if he did, somebody would probably end up crippled or dead, so he gave Jed a job painting x marks on the trees that were to be cut. Jed would work doing the painting until early afternoon, then he would return to his farm and deal with the animals.

Now all that loving stuff that Jed had said in the barn before he had to get married was only something that he had heard form Dale Clemens. He knew nothing of the sort and Virginia also drew a blank on the subject. In the year that the two had been married, they celebrated their anniversary, but they had never really consummated their marriage and did not know how.

Over the year they had talked several times about how nice it would be to have some kids that they could think of as their younger brothers and sisters, being they were the babies of their families. Jed figured it would not hurt to have a boy that could help him around the farm. He felt with both jobs he could use the help. The only problem with the conversation was when they got to the how, neither of them knew.

Virginia had remembered that she thought she had heard someone speak of a bird they called a stork and how the bird would bring the baby to the house on a certain night. Each time she would get close enough to try and make out the conversation better, one of her parents would run her back to her room. She never obtained the correct information about the bird.

Virginia had heard about Santa Clause and he had visited their home many times when she was a little girl. She figured maybe he would have the answer. However, Jed had never heard of Santa Clause. Virginia spent hours explaining the Santa Clause story to Jed. He knew the guy had never visited his house before and he knew that if the bearded guy tried coming down their chimney the sisters would have burned him up.

"So you never got a Christmas present?" Virginia asked her husband. Jed looked pitiful with his big, sad blue eyes. "I didn't get nothing. We didn't even put no tree in the house. I guess that is why he never came," Jed explained. Virginia felt sorry for Jed and reached over and hugged his neck. Jed didn't know what to do about that. He just figured his wife was doing something strange. He felt that she was a little dumb about certain things. He knew that hugging people was what you did just before you left.

"Jed, I got an idea about how we can find out about how to order us a baby from that stork. Christmas is coming soon and we can write Santa a letter asking him for the information as to how we can contact that stork and order us a baby. We will have to write him anyhow and tell him what we want for Christmas," Virginia explained. Jed looked disappointed. "I don't know how to write," Jed said. Virginia smiled at Jed. "I know how to write, but you can help me figure out what we are going to say to Santa," Virginia explained. Jed was thrilled that she was going to include him in with something as sophisticated as writing a letter to the great Santa. He could not wait to ask this Santa guy about the baby stuff and also ask him to bring him some toys. He was so happy that he had a good wife that knew all the great things.

They wasted no time. That night they sat down and wrote a letter to Santa Clause. In the letter they asked about the stork and how they could make contact with this bird. Virginia asked for a bicycle as she had never had one before. Jed asked for one of those shiny red wagons that he had never got when he was a kid. He felt that maybe the wagon would help him do things around the farm.

The next day Virginia did something that she had never done before. She rode with Jed into town on the mule to mail the letter to Santa Clause. Of course she had never addressed a letter that had ever gone out to Santa and she did not have an address. Jed figured that the post office would know those things. He assured her that they would help them with that problem.

Now the town people had seen many things happen in the small town. They were not ready for this day and to see Virginia on a mule with Jed Ledbetter. Everyone watched as they got down from the old mule. They were amazed. Jed and Virginia entered the post office and both looked suspicious as they approached the counter, where a young sneaky looking man was waiting to help them.

Virginia was a shy girl and had not asked many questions to strangers. She had been taught against doing those such things. Jed stepped in front of his wife. "Reckon you can give us an address where we can put it on this envelope that is going to the North Pole?" Jed questioned the young man. The man grinned real big as he took the letter out of Jed's hand. He looked closely at the letter and took it to the back of the room where another young man was working. They talked for a short time and the young man returned to the counter.

"I think we can take care of this for you. I talked with my friend and he knows the address to where Santa lives at his workshop. We will see that it gets to him," the young man explained. Jed and Virginia smiled brightly. They thanked the young man and walked out of the post office.

Jed and Virginia did not realize that the other young man at the back of the room was Dale Clemens and he had more tricks up his sleeve than leaves on the ground in fall. The letter would be read by someone, but not the great Santa Clause. The two boys were going to have a time and for Dale Clemens, it would be his second time around with Jed.

A week had passed since they had mailed the letter to Santa. Virginia had watched the mail box everyday. On this day the letter finally came. She waited about opening it until Jed came in from marking trees. "Jed, the letter form Santa came today in the mail," she informed her husband. He was ecstatic. He could hardly wait to find out what was in the letter. "Open it and read it to me," Jed said.

Virginia opened the letter and it explained everything that they needed to know about summoning the stork to their home. Jed was amazed at how easy it was to get a baby. They planned to go to town that day and fulfill the requirement for getting the baby. It was a simple plan and they did not have to do too much to make it happen. All they had to do was go to town, take off all their cloths, lie down in the middle of the road in town and yell as loud as they could, "Here we are stork. Come and give us a baby", and then start licking each others faces.

Of course that night Wade Haney had to go to the local police department and bail out his daughter and son-in-law. He couldn't have been more embarrassed than if he would have worn a dress to town. The entire town had seen the couple and the scandal had reached the whole community. Everyone thought Jed had begun to rub off on Virginia.

On the way home from the police department Wade had him a conversation with his daughter and Jed. "Why would you two do something like this to me after all I done for you two," Wade scolded. Virginia had been silent, but now she was mad. "We didn't do anything that you and momma didn't do. You had to do that to get the stork to come and bring us," she informed her father. Jed said, "Yea". Virginia explained the entire Santa thing to her father and about how they were trying to get him a grandbaby.

At that very moment Wade realized something that had not dawned on him over the past year. He realized that his daughter and Jed were really innocent of what he had accused them of the year before. He was confused and did not know what to say or do. His daughter knew nothing about life and childbearing and his son-in-law knew even less. They had been innocent in the beginning and they were still innocent in the end. Wade could not believe that he had forced his youngest daughter to get married and he could not believe that he had forced a boy with mental problems to marry his daughter.

Wade Haney made a quick stop at the preacher's house to talk it over with him. The preacher informed Wade that it was too late to try and get the marriage annulled. They had been married too long. Wade thanked the preacher for his help and continued on his journey home with the two kids. He knew that he had messed up and now the outcome could not be corrected. He would just have to make the best of things.

They arrived at Wade's house and Wade explained to his wife everything that had conspired over the night. She too was devastated at the knowledge about the couple. Virginia's mother, Betty, assured her husband that she would explain the facts to her daughter so her daughter would have a better understanding of how grown-up things worked. They had both agreed that Betty would tell Virginia everything about the birds and the bees, while Wade told Jed the same thing. They figured that was the least they could do.

Betty summoned Virginia to go with her into another room so she could do the explaining, while Wade would tell Jed. The only problem there was that when Wade had set Jed down in a chair, he realized that there would be no way that he could ever get Jed to understand what he was saying to him. Wade decided to talk about work instead. He figure that was something important that the boy would need to know worse. He explained that when somebody was talking to him, he needed to do just exactly what they say to do and don't ask any questions as to why they want him to do that. Wade explained that if he followed all of the directions he would make a good worker.

After the conversations were over Wade took the couple back to their own house. He let them know that he would get the old mule they had left in town and bring it over to them. They said their farewells, and then Wade Haney parted. It was only about ten o' clock at night and Virginia was armed with some new knowledge. She was about to spring it on Jed about how babies came into the world. She figured she would do just exactly what her mother had told her to do. For the first time she realized what the big fuss was about when her father had found Jed laying across her in the barn.

Jed was in the kitchen fixing him some coffee. Virginia had slipped off into her bedroom and put on something more comfortable. When she was ready she called out, "Jed, I got something to show you. Come into my bedroom". She was going to give Jed the biggest surprise of his life. She was amazed at why she had felt certain feelings for Jed when they were real close. Now she knew what all those feelings had been about.

Jed had his cup of coffee in his hand when he entered the bedroom and saw Virginia with a skimpy outfit on. Jed dropped the cup to the floor and it broke. Virginia's sister, Beth, had been in the room when her mother was explaining the details about marriage to the youngest daughter.

Beth gave Virginia the skimpy outfit to wear. Beth was the other daughter that was part of the shotgun wedding. She too figured that she might be able to explain the situation better so Virginia would have a greater understanding than her mother could explain.

When Jed seen his wife in the new outfit, he could hardly breath. He was surprised that they made such things for girls. He had also wondered if they made such things for boys too. If he would have known that information at an earlier time, he would have asked that Santa guy for one or maybe two.

He felt that Virginia and he could take turns looking at each other in that mirror thing he had found.

Virginia was going to tell Jed all about what she had learned at her parent's house. The only difference was that she was going to explain it in the only way her husband could understand. She was going to use the visual effect on Jed. "Jed, I want you to take all of your clothes off and then I will tell you what to do. You will need to remember some of what daddy told you, and then we can get us a baby," Virginia explained.

Jed took all of his clothes off, except his boots. "Ok, here I am now tell me what to do," Jed said. Virginia smiled at him wickedly and said, "Ok Jed, now do what daddy told you to do and let's go to town," Virginia explained. Why that was all it took for Jed. He was ready to do exactly what his wife told him to do.

The Chief of Police was walking around the town that night when he noticed something was not right. Jed was in the middle of the street with nothing on but a pair of boots. He rushed over to where Jed was standing. "Boy, I thought I already arrested you once today for doing that," the chief said. Jed looked strait at the chief. "No sir. You arrested me earlier this evening for trying to call the stork to bring us a baby," Jed explained. The Chief of Police looked weary at having to deal with Jed twice on the same day. "Why are you dressed like that, Jed?" the chief asked. Jed smiled and said, "My wife said that we were going to town and I guess I beat her here. You hadn't seen her have you?" Jed asked.

After Wade Haney had made his second embarrassing trip for the night to the police department to get Jed, he returned home again. Betty was mad by now. She had thought Wade explained everything to Jed. "You said that we would both have to do that. I was so embarrassed telling Virginia what I had to tell her and here you were not telling Jed anything," Betty said. Virginia had one brother named "Sam". He had found out what was going on and decided to take Jed outside and give him the real facts of life.

"You don't say. You don't mean all of that with boys and girls. Why I have never heard any likes of that in my entire life. My sisters never mentioned a thing about stuff such as that," Jed rattled on. Sam informed Jed that everything he said was the whole truth and that if he followed the directions, he would be a father. Sam took Jed back to Jed's place where Virginia had been waiting for hours. She had realized that Jed might have misunderstood what she had told him. Jed was fully aware now.

Within two months it was December and Virginia was pregnant with a baby. However, the entire situation had not been explained fully to Jed. He thought that when Virginia had said she was going to have a baby, she meant now. He had went out to the barn and gathered up some of his tools. His plan was to teach his son how to work just as soon as his son came out. Over the two month period Virginia had been informed about many things and she knew that it was going to take more time than Jed had realized.

After Virginia informed her husband that it took nine months for a baby to be fully made, he was shocked. "Well I can make one in that amount of time," Jed informed his wife. Of course she convinced him that the reason that it took so long was kind of on the same line as the story about taking the biscuits out of the oven too soon. Jed remembered the story that his mother told him before she died. He had slipped into the kitchen and pulled a piece of raw dough off one of the biscuits. She caught him and explained that the dough was not done and he could get worms. Jed did not want a wormy baby so he figured Virginia was right and should not be rushed.

Virginia still believed in Santa Clause and it was now Christmas Eve, however, Jed had been fooled too many times over the past few years. He was still uncertain about the Santa Clause guy. He still kept his hopes high that the man would come and bring them gifts. "Reckon we should put out the fire in the fireplace?" Jed asked. "No, we never had to put it out when we were at home. I remember asking daddy the same thing and he said that Santa was fireproof," explained Virginia.

Now this was a night when fate could run wildly and at the Ledbetter house it did. It seems that some of the men Jed worked with were nice enough to provide Jed with some Christmas decorations for the tree. While Jed was bringing some of the decorations into the house, he overlooked a small bell that he had dropped on the ground. At the Ledbetter farm many of the chickens and roosters roamed free. Jed did not notice when one of the roosters accidentally got the bell hung onto one of the spurs on the rooster's leg. The old rooster ran off with the jingling bell.

It was late at night when Jed and Virginia decided to go to bed. They had been in the bed for about thirty minutes when a new noise came to their ears. Jed rose up in the bed and strained his ears to try and hear what it was that suddenly came to his attention. "What is it?" Virginia questioned. Jed slowly turned toward Virginia and said, "There's a something a coming. I can hear it," Jed answered.

Both listened closely. Jingle, jingle, jingle came the noise. Virginia heard the sound. "What is making that kind of noise?" she asked. Jed shushed her so he could hear. The sound moved closer, and then went from the ground to the top of the house.

"Don't move, Virginia. It's Santa and Ima hearing those deer of his. It's just like you said. Those deer are wearing them bells." He told Virginia. They both sat quietly and the noise continued on into the night, until morning. Jed and Virginia never closed their eyes once during the night. "Jed, why do you think Santa stayed all night on our roof?" Virginia questioned. "I don't know. Maybe he was putting them presents under our tree and slipped and fell. He could be hurt," Jed explained to Virginia. She gave Jed a curious glance.

Suddenly, the jingle sound came again and this time they heard urururururrrrrr. The sound startled the both of them, but they realized the sound was that of a rooster. Jed jumped out of bed and ran outside. The old rooster sat perched on top of the house. It moved and made the jingle noise. Jed noticed the tiny bell that was attached to the rooster's foot.

After a short while, he came back into the house and looked under their tree, and then and returned to his bed where Virginia awaited him. "What was it, Jed" Virginia asked. Jed looked mad. "That Santa Feller is something else. He came last night, but didn't leave us anything. I think he was trying to steal one of our roosters," Jed explained. Virginia looked puzzled. "How do you know he was trying to steal our roosters?" she asked. Jed looked real serious.

"Well, he was either trying to steal our roosters or he has stopped using them deer and started using roosters to fly with, cause one of them deer bells is hung up on a red rooster that looks a lot like ours." Jed explained. Virginia jumped up and ran to look under the tree. There was nothing, just like Jed had told her. Santa had come and he left nothing. She was heartbroken and started to cry.

Now Jed had never been a very passionate man as he had very little passion for the sisters that always aggravated him. However, he felt something strange inside and he realized that he did not like hearing Virginia cry.

Jed rushed outside to the barn and in only a few minutes he was back with something wrapped up in an old newspaper that he found. He gave it to Virginia. She stopped crying and looked at Jed. "What is it?" Virginia asked. He motioned for her to open the newspaper and see. She opened the newspaper and a very pretty box was beneath the paper. She opened the box and a ballerina popped up and music began to play. She looked up at Jed and a big smile ran all the way across her face. She liked the gift and that made Jed happy.

He had found the box when he was cleaning out the old Miller house. He had saved the box and was going to use it to store small screws and nails in. he knew that it seemed girly, but he did not mind. Jed now felt that the box should be used by Virginia. He had fallen in love and he felt that Virginia should have the box. She hugged Jed and gave him a big kiss.

Wade and Betty Haney knew that Virginia still believed in Santa Clause and they had not forgotten. Later in the day they dropped by and informed Jed and Virginia that Santa had mistakenly left the presents for them at their house. Jed and Virginia went home with Wade and Betty. It was the first time that Jed had ever had a Christmas. After that day he believed in Santa and could hardly wait until the next Christmas.

Months rolled by since Christmas and Virginia was getting huge. She was one month past due on delivering her child. Jed was getting concerned. He had done everything that Virginia had wanted him to do. He waited on her hand and foot and thought how funny it had been only a few years back when he thought that Virginia would be the one waiting on him hand and foot.

Jed only made a very small amount of money at his job with Wade. He could not afford a doctor for Virginia, but the family doctor was aware of the situation and informed Wade that he would not charge for his services. He had been the family doctor all of Virginia's life. He had brought her into the world when Betty was pregnant with Virginia. The doctor was proud to be delivering a baby for Virginia. He only hoped that the baby received its health from Jed and Virginia and not its brains. He knew that only time would tell.

Now the old doctor was also concerned about Virginia. She had gained too much weight for a single child birth. He was already suspicious that there could be twins come form this birth. However, he was worried that there might be complications from the birth. That information he kept to himself. He had planned on a nurse to come and help him with the delivery when the time came. She had agreed to be there.

It was on the fourth day of July when the doctor was summoned to the Ledbetter home. Virginia was having pains in her stomach and the doctor could only assume that it was time. He tried to make contact with the nurse, but she had left the area to spend the holiday with her parents, which lived in another county. The doctor arrived and was preparing for a home delivery. He was getting things setup in the bedroom when he called Jed into the room.

Sam Haney was still out trying to round up his parents to let them know of the coming birth. They had planned to go up into the woods to a good fishing and camping spot that Wade always liked. The only problem was that the place was at least a half-day hike and Betty would not make it back in time.

"Jed, you're going to have to help me with this delivery of your child. I will tell you what you have to do," the doctor explained. Jed was scared. He had never done anything like that before in his life. "Doctor, can't we put this off until Virginia's mother gets here?" the doctor looked at Jed solemnly. "No, this is not by choice. You have to help me or I am in big trouble," the doctor explained. Jed started walking back and fourth across the floor.

"Why don't you and me go to town and have us a beer first," Jed said. The doctor gave Jed a sour look and motioned him over. "Maybe we can go get one after the baby is born. We can take him with us," Jed said as he moved to the doctor. "I will need you to do exactly what I tell you to do when the time comes," the doctor informed Jed. Jed shook his head in agreement. "I will need a few more blankets. Go get them for me," the doctor demanded. Jed moved quickly out of the room.

Jed looked all through the house to find all of the blankets. He had gathered several before returning back to the bedroom where the doctor and Virginia were. By the time he reached the bedroom something was happening. Virginia was screaming and the doctor was yelling at her to push. Jed did not know what to do. He dropped the blankets in the floor and walked over to the bed. The doctor yelled for her to push again. Jed looked at Virginia and yelled, "Push Virginia, push." "Shut up, Jed!" Virginia screamed back.

Virginia pushed one last time and the baby came out in the doctor's hands. Jed was surprised. He had somehow thought that the baby would be born with some kind of clothing on. He had hoped the clothing would be overhauls like he wore. "Doctor, we been cheated. That baby is filthy and naked," Jed said. The doctor thumped the baby on its tail to try and make it cry out. Jed looked at the doctor and said, "Doctor, I'm the daddy and I'm the one who supposed to be whipping the baby, but I didn't see anything he did wrong."

The doctor had not heard the baby cry and he turned to Jed. "Get me another lamp so I can see more clearly!" the doctor demanded. Jed moved quickly and lit a new lamp. He moved to the doctor and tried to give the doctor the lamp. "You'll need to hold it for me," the doctor said. Jed did what he was told.

The doctor used one of those big nose bulbs to try and suction the baby's mouth. He thumped the baby again and it still did not cry. "What's wrong with the baby?" Jed asked. At that point Virginia became aware that something was wrong. She tried to move to the end of the bed. "Stay where you are, Virginia" the doctor said. "What's wrong with my baby?" she insisted. The doctor did not answer, but he noticed another problem had arisen. He moved the baby to the corner of the room and gently placed it in the floor, and then returned to the foot of the bed. This concerned Jed.

"Hey, why is the baby not talking?" Jed asked as he moved to with the light toward where the baby had been placed. "Come back with that light!" the doctor ordered. Jed stopped and turned toward the doctor. "Hey, the baby's over here. Why would you want me to come back over there?" Jed asked inquisitively. "Because there is another one coming," the doctor answered.

"What do you mean another?" Jed asked. "I mean come back here with the light because another baby is about to be born," the doctor explained. Jed looked more confused. He turned and looked at Virginia. "Who else you been doing that secret thing with that your brother told me to do to get this baby? I've been cheated on," Jed said.

"You've not been cheated on, Jed. Some women have more than one baby at a time," the doctor explained to Jed. Now Jed was really confused. About that time the doctor pulled another baby from Virginia. It too was a boy like the first. He thumped it on its tail and this time the biggest scream came from the baby. The noise was so loud that it hurt Jed's ears. Jed looked at Virginia and said, "That baby has got your voice when you are mad".

The doctor said to Jed, "What are you going to name this child?" Jed thought for a moment and said, "Well, we were going to name the first child "Leroy", but now I don't know what to name this surprise child," Jed said. The doctor placed the baby beside its mother and returned to the foot of the bed. Jed was moving toward the front of the bed when the doctor grabbed him by his collar and pulled him back to the foot of the bed. "Not so fast, Jed. We still have another one that is being born," Jed looked like he had been hit by a tree. He thought for a moment and started moving away from the bed with the light.

"I still need that light, Jed," the doctor said. Jed stopped and slowly walked back to the foot of the bed. "Doctor, I can't afford to have anymore of those babies, and I think that those babies might be looking for the light so they can get out. We didn't really want them all right now so I'm just gonna turn the light off so they will know that now is not the time and they will go back and wait until we decide to have another baby," Jed explained to the doctor. The doctor gave Jed a crazy look and said, "Son, don't you understand. This is not a choice. God gave these babies to you and he expects you to except them". Jed shook his head in disbelief. "Well I hope god's got some instructions with them for Virginia to read cause I don't know what to do with all those babies and I don't know how to read," Jed said.

Within a very short period of time the doctor had received four babies from Virginia. He was amazed and smiling. Jed was not and he was frowning. "I guess I can see why you so happy, doctor. We are the ones that are gonna starve," Jed informed the doctor as he moved next to his wife. Virginia took Jed by his hand and smiled up at him. Moments later a noise began to come from the corner of the room where the first baby had been placed. The noise went, "Brrrrrrmmm". Jed and Virginia noticed the sound and stopped talking. The noise came again, but this time it was much louder. "Brrrrrmmmmmm!!!" the noise came again. Jed looked at the doctor to see if he noticed, and then turned to Virginia and said, "That baby is haunting us". A bad smell followed the noise this time and stifled Jed. Again, Jed heard, "Brrrrmmmmmmaaah!" and said to Virginia, "That baby is a haunting and a stinking us".

The doctor moved to where he had placed the first child. He picked up the child and started cleaning out the baby's mouth. "This baby is not dead. It is breathing and breaking wind," said the doctor. Jed was surprised, but he seemed contented that they were to have four children. He reached down and said to Virginia, "You sure are some woman. You can give us an entire family with one doing. We gonna starve to death, but we gonna have us some fun while we do".

A total of three boys and one girl were delivered that night. The Wade Family finally arrived at the house and was shocked at the fact that they were now the grandparents of four babies. They had given all four babies names before the night was over. The first boy would be called Bubba. The second would be called Vern. The third would be called Leroy, and the fourth baby was a girl. She would be called Betty Lou.

Jed had given Bubba that name because the old mule had kicked him hard one day. Jed looked at the mule and said, "You gonna get it, Bubba". Jed figured the first born was leading the way for the other three and that was one more kick in the butt for him.

The doctor was amazed. He knew that Jed and Virginia had a habit of causing the people around the community to talk. This night would give them something very big to talk about. It might even scare the majority of the community by allowing them to think that there were four more Jed and Virginia's that were born on this night. The doctor felt that would be some real good scandal for the community.

Wade and Betty Haney could hardly believe what had happened. They figured that the children being born on the Fourth of July was some kind of omen. They could only hope that the children would not grow up to be like their parents. Now the Haney family meant no harm by those thoughts. They just figured that one Jed and one Virginia would be all the family could handle. They also felt a little guilty for explaining the birds and the bees to the only two real children in town. They now felt that was a big mistake for everyone.

Of course the Haney's knew that since they were responsible, they should do their best to try and help the couple as much as they could with the kids. Wade knew that it would be a nightmare made on earth and he should spend a lot more time at work. He guessed that more work would also mean more pay and he knew that he was going to have to give his son-in-law a very large raise to help with the babies.

Wade Haney knew that Jed was probably going to be the most well paid tree marker in the world. Unfortunately, he knew that Betty would not let him live down the problem that he caused by forcing his youngest daughter into marrying Jed Ledbetter. On the other hand, Virginia was proud that she did marry Jed. He had become her husband and she loved him. He had been the only person to make her happy. She had come to realize that if she would have married one of those other boys at school; she might have missed all the adventure that Jed was ready and able to give to her. The world would just have to wonder why.

Chapter Four

Raising Bubba

Now if you have ever tried to raise children, you know without the proper knowledge things could get pretty scary. It could have looked a lot like Halloween at the Ledbetter house and Bubba was the scariest baby of them all. Three of the Ledbetter babies came into life with their lungs in overdrive, but Bubba did not. He was determined to be the silence before the storm. For Jed and Virginia, he was the storm.

Bubba was determined to undermine the new knowledge of child rearing that was suddenly bestowed upon Virginia and Jed. He had an ulterior motive for being born that the other three babies did not have. He did not know what that was at the moment, but he was sure that he would eventually find out. The other three took to the bottle quiet well. Bubba did not. Bubba was stubborn about everything and the other three were not.

Bubba was now eight hours old and had finally decided to cry. He cried and cried. Jed figured that if he gave him a bottle it would automatically stop. Not Bubba. He wanted something that Jed or Virginia knew not what. He would not take the bottle from Jed and Jed refused to allow Virginia to try and feed him. Jed had heard that when baby chicks first opens their eyes after birth, it becomes attached to whom it first seen. Jed knew that he wanted Bubba to be attached to him and he was set on taking care of Bubba until he opened his eyes and seen him.

"Jed, just let me feed him this one time so he will shut up. I have never heard a baby cry as loud as Bubba," said Virginia. Jed jumped to his feet with Bubba in his arms. "If he sees you, I won't be worth poop to him. I'll go and fix him another bottle. Maybe I didn't put enough milk in the last one," Jed informed Virginia. He walked into the kitchen where the old wood stove had been busy earlier heating the milk for the other babies. Jed poured some more milk into the iron pot. Every move Jed made, Bubba would cry in unison to Jed's footsteps.

Within a few minutes the milk was at boiling point. He had been informed earlier by Betty Haney that the milk must be boiled every time. Jed poured the glass baby bottle full of milk and moved the iron pot to the middle of the wood stove. "Ok, Bubba. You gonna drink this bottle this time," Jed said, and then pushed the bottle right up to Bubba's mouth. Jed waited patiently for Bubba to take his milk. Bubba locked his jaws shut and would not let Jed get the bottle between his locked lips.

Jed had not paid much attention to Betty when she was explaining the ups and downs of the baby bottle. The first thing that he forgot was that the bottle must be cooled after the boiling. Jed sometimes just heard bits and pieces of a conversation and Virginia had not noticed that Jed had not cooled the bottle.

Jed was mad and he threw the bottle on the floor, causing the glass to break all over the floor. "Jed, you better not be getting mad at that little baby," said Virginia. "He aint no little baby. He can cry louder and harder than I ever could. I'm getting mad at myself cause I just threw the bottle to the floor and now Ima gonna have to go outside to the barn and milk ole Betsy again. I'm not gonna leave Bubba here with you either cause I know you'll feed him and he'll see you first," Jed said.

Jed went outside and made his way to the barn with Bubba. He knew he had to find the milking pot so he could milk Betsy. Jed laid the screaming Bubba down in some hay near Betsy while he looked for the pan. After only a short spell, Jed noticed that Bubba had stopped crying. Jed thought that maybe Bubba had died so he ran over to where he had left Bubba.

When Jed saw what was happening, he fell to his knees. "Oh my god! Bubba don't look!" Jed screamed as he tried to pry Bubba away from the cow. Jed worked hard, but Bubba had a strong grip on Betsy. It seems that Betsy had moved close to Bubba and somehow Bubba found his lunch and he was draining Betsy dry of her milk. Jed finally gave up and let Bubba have his way. Jed was heart broken.

After Bubba finished his meal, Jed was able to bring Bubba back to the house. Jed was crying something furiously and Bubba was just silent. Virginia had thought

Jed had got mad again and actually done something to Bubba. She ran quickly up to Jed and grabbed Bubba away from Jed. Bubba looked contented and happy. He had found what he wanted and it did not matter to him at the time that Jed was upset.

"You might as well take the boy. He's been had by Betsy. He seen her and now he's her little man," Jed explained as he wiped the tears from his eyes. Virginia was extremely confused about the situation and feared to ask what had happened, but she had a weakness when it came to knowing about something strange. Of course that is why she was in the predicament that she found herself in on that day.

"What are you talking about, Jed?" she questioned. He looked down into Virginia's arms at Bubba. "Ima talking about him. He caught me with my head turned and made Betsy feed him. I saw those beady eyes of his look straight at Betsy. He took to her right quickly. You don't hear him crying none anymore, do ya?" Jed asked. Virginia was still puzzled. "What does all that mean, Jed?" she questioned. Jed shrugged his shoulders and looked sadly into Virginia's eyes. "I guess it means that he loves ole Betsy better than he loves either of us," Jed explained. Virginia hugged her husband and assured him that ever what had happened would in the end be for the good of the family.

Things did not get better from that point on. They kind of went straight down the hill. It seems that Bubba did like ole Betsy after that. He would not touch the bottle. Jed had to take him out to the barn to see Betsy five and six times a day. On occasions, neighbors would drop by to visit with Jed and Virginia, but was shocked and stopped coming after they seen the way Bubba was fed. Jed didn't make any bones about hiding the fact either. Sometimes he would just bring ole Betsy in the house while the neighbors were visiting and let Bubba feed straight from the cow, right in front of the neighbors.

Virginia was embarrassed by Bubba, but she decided that it was a natural thing for people to want fresh things. She had not been able to breast feed any of the babies and she felt that meant they all should at least have the right to fend for themselves. She felt that maybe Jed should have had some extra manners around the neighbors.

The town really hated seeing the Ledbetter family enter the city limits. They knew that the day would be a brand new experience for them. Jed had got his hands on a wagon so Bubba the mule could pull them all to town. Sometimes Jed would have ole Betsy tied to the back of the wagon. It would all depend on if they were going to be in town a while. Jed would stop the wagon on the side of the street and let Bubba crawl under Betsy and feed.

There was a man passing through town one day and noticed baby Bubba beneath Betsy and the man had thought the child had been run over by the cow. He stopped and dragged Bubba out from under Betsy. Bubba was mad as a hornet about that. He cried like there were no tomorrow. Sometimes Virginia would talk Jed into bringing a sheet along with them and covering Betsy up so Bubba could crawl under without anyone seeing.

Jed had gotten tired of going out at night so Bubba could feed, so he started bringing Betsy into the house to sleep beside the bed. Bubba would cry and Jed would just stick Bubba under Betsy and the silence would come. Virginia was not too pleased about that. She had to clean and mop the bedroom floor everyday. She argued with Jed continuously about bringing Betsy into the house. Jed compromised by tying Betsy just outside the bedroom window. Bubba would cry and Jed would hold him out the window and let him feed. Bubba got good at that position and really could have been an acrobat later in life. He could make all the moves to get into the position to feed.

Jed was proud of Bubba for many of his new acrobatic moves. Jed would sometimes share those memories with some of his co-workers and they just sit there with their mouths wide open. They did not know how to respond to Jed and they really didn't want to. Wade Haney would never look at the other men in the eyes again. He would always talk to them with his head turned away. Jed never thought once about telling the men everything about anything that happened. Wade Haney always wished for the lunch breaks to be over quickly.

Wade had argued time and time again with Betty about why Jed had to work with them. "There should be some kind of job the boy could do," Wade argued. Betty would only get mad. "If you are talking about getting rid of Jed again, think twice. You did this to those poor kids. If it had not been for you and your mistaken thoughts, our daughter would probably be married to someone else. You made the bed and it is stinky. Now you are just going to have to sleep in the crap that he rubbed all over that bed," Betty would tell her husband.

There it was right back in his face just like it had happened yesterday. He would never live down what he had done and wished many a time that he would have bought Jed several new guns and called it even. Many times he wished Virginia would have just got pregnant and never married Jed at all. He could have lived much better with the momentary disgrace against his family name as to live with that disgrace everyday.

At the end of the day Wade and Betty were thankful for their grandchildren and that Jed was at least a decent man in his own way. He might have been missing certain things in the head, but he was still good to their daughter. That was important to them. That would be an important thing in the future. Jed was kinfolk.

Chapter Five

The Language Barrier

It seems that the Ledbetter kids were growing like wild Kudzu in a field. Bubba was late in learning how to talk. He had been running around and playing before he said his first word, which was Betsy. When he did get to talking, the problem was not how much he could speak, but what it was that was going to be coming out of his mouth. It also was a matter of who was around when those things did come out of his mouth.

It seems that Bubba had a way with colorful metaphors and loved to use foul language often. He thought it was a natural thing to do. With Bubba, many things that looked natural to him did not look that natural to others. The cussing had become a great big problem for Jed and Virginia as they had finally got the neighbors to stop talking about Bubba and Betsy. They had hoped they could go back to being just a redneck family, instead of a redneck family the redneck neighbors looked down on. Many times Jed or Virginia would hear one of the neighbors that had been in jail say, "Look at those idiots". Of course hearing someone that was morally not fit say those things hurt much worse than normal.

Bubba was seven and had started to teach Vern some of his bad language. Sometimes the neighbors would be over at the house and both of the boys would go to saying bad words in unison. Virginia tried everything to stop the boys from cussing. "I am going to wash your little mouths out with some soap," Virginia would tell them. They would look so seriously at her and say, "Yes ma". They really meant well, but only for a minute.

One of Virginia's friends from church had a parrot that would quote religious scriptures. Everyone loved to see that bird and hear what words of wisdom he was going to say today. The friend was going out of town and offered to pay Virginia if she would watch the bird until she returned. It was only going to be for a few days and Virginia knew that they needed the money. She agreed to do it. After Bubba and Vern finished with the bird, the only thing that it would say was, "Go to hell son of a bitch". The friend was furious. Virginia was apologetic that her boys had done wrong with the bird. The friend finally had to take the bird to church and have the members pray for the bird. It was never right again.

Jed and Virginia was at the end of their rope, when Virginia's mother advised her that the preacher knew much about helping in those type matters. She had scheduled an appointment with the preacher for Virginia to take the boys over to see him. Virginia had taken the boys to church as often as she could, but they still had no clear understanding of god. Jed would do his best to try and get the boys to understand about god. However, his understanding was much different than others.

Jed would sometimes hide in the boy's closet at night and try to scare the boys into not cussing. He would change his voice to a deep voice and say, "This is god and if you say a bad word again, Ima gonna git you". Bubba and Vern would just laugh at him. One time they beat Jed to the draw. They had hid under some covers in the closet and Jed slipped into the closet to scare the boys. He settled in and said in a deep voice, "This is god. If you two don't quit your cussing, Ima gonna git you real good". Moments later, Bubba and Vern said in a low voice from beneath the hidden covers, "You a lying. I'm God". Jed was frightened and ran out of the closet as fast as he could. He never did sneak into the dark closet again.

The day came when Virginia met with the preacher and brought Bubba and Vern with her. He said that he would need to speak to each one separately. He wanted to take Vern in first, being that Vern was the youngest and the preacher felt that he could have the best success with him. Virginia was a little apprehensive about letting her child go. She wanted him to be a better child, but she was not aware of how the preacher was going to handle the situation. She did not want her child to be damaged and not have a desire to ever go to church again.

The preacher took Vern into his office and closed the door behind him. He sat Vern right down in a chair and asked Vern sternly, "Where is god?" Vern did not respond. He just looked down at his hands so the preacher raised his voice even more and shook his finger in Vern's face. "I said where is god?" Again Vern did not respond and the preacher raised his voice even louder at Vern. "Where is God I say?" he questioned Vern with great vigor.

Suddenly, Vern was so scared that he ran out of the office and passed where Bubba was sitting. Bubba got up and ran after him. He did not catch Vern until they reached the farm and Vern immediately ran into the closet. Bubba followed and closed the door. Bubba could tell that something bad had happened to Vern. Normally Vern had small eyes, but on this day they were so large that Bubba could see them even in the dark closet.

"What happened, Vern?" Bubba questioned excitedly. Vern was breathing hard and could barely catch his breath. Bubba shook Vern and asked him again what had happened. Still, Vern was not responsive to Bubba's questioning.

Finally, Bubba told Vern that if he did not tell him, he would go out of the closet and lock him in all by himself. Vern gave in and finally said, "We in big trouble this time. You and me both are and they gonna pin it all on us".

Bubba looked confused. His brother was making no sense at all to him. "What are you talking about, stupid? Why are we in trouble?" Bubba asked in a concerned voice. Vern just shook his head. "Don't you know? God's a missing and they thank we did it. They probably gonna hang us or something," Vern replied. Bubba was stunned. He didn't know what to say to his brother.

That visit with the preacher seemed to have stopped Vern from his cussing, but had very little effect on Bubba. He seemed to get worse and worse. Jed had several long talks with Bubba behind the wood shed, but that still had no great effect on Bubba's new language. He just cussed more, but not around Jed as often.

One day Jed asked one of the men that he logged with about what he should do about Bubba's cussing. The logger thought about the problem all day. At the end of the day, he told Jed a possible answer to the problem. "Christmas is coming, Jed. You could ask Bubba what it is he wants for Christmas. If he cusses while he tells you, leave a pile of dog crap in place of the gift or gifts he asked for. Jed, that should teach him that Santa Clause would not like what he is saying," the logger informed Jed.

Jed shook his head in agreement. "That could work, but we really have a problem with that Santa Fella. It seems he keeps leaving all of our goodies at Wade and Betty's house. Virginia and I have waited up for him every Christmas Eve for the past few years and he has not showed himself at our house," Jed explained. The logger looked at Jed bewildered and turned and walked away. Jed knew that it would be worth a try. He could just trick Bubba into thinking that Santa was going to come to their house this time on Christmas and leave him some goodies.

As soon as Jed got home he could not wait to tell Virginia about the plan. He explained in detail everything that the logger had told him to do. Jed informed Virginia that they would have to purchase some gifts for the kids and pretend that Santa had brought them. She made Jed promise her that if they did do that they would buy Bubba some gifts so he would not feel left out and be mad at the other kids. Jed reluctantly agreed and the plan was set.

That night they informed all of the kids that Santa Clause was coming to their house this time and if they had been bad he would not leave them anything. Bubba kept his eye on his parents. He was not sure if he should believe the things he had heard. "Ok pa, you gonna make us stay up all night to see him and he just aint gonna come," Bubba said. Just jumped up from his seat and said, "Bubba, if you try staying up all night for Santa, he will leave you nothing. Only if you'd be good and not cuss will you get something," Jed told him. Bubba agreed that he would not cuss anymore and if Santa would go ahead and give an advance and not leave him out on the Christmas presents this year, he would not cuss again.

Jed sent the other children to Virginia to tell her what they wanted while he sat Bubba down beside him. "Bubba, what do you want Santa Clause to bring you?" Jed asked. Bubba looked up at the ceiling and said, " Just tell that damn Santa Clause man that I would like a damn train set and a damn wagon like those other damn kids at the end of the road," replied Bubba. Jed looked upset. He knew that he would have to execute the plan that had been made. "Well git on down and go on. It'll be up to the Santa fella," Jed told Bubba as he pushed Bubba from the couch.

Jed stayed on the couch and sat there recounting his past several years with Bubba. Bubba had caused so many problems. It wasn't bad enough that he had to take Bubba to the barn for feeding several times a day. Eventually Bubba was cussing ole Betsy for being out of milk. Bubba even told Jed that he should just shoot her because she was not worth nothing if she could not feed him. Bubba really loved Betsy and was only saying those things to Jed. One day Jed got tired of hearing Bubba saying that and Jed loaded his shotgun and headed to the barn. Bubba was crying something awful at the thought that Jed was really going to do it.

A week had passed and it was Christmas Eve. Jed knew that since Bubba had cussed each time that he asked for one of the presents, he would leave some dog crap with a name tag for Bubba. Jed made all of the kids go to bed early. Virginia had been to town and bought some presents that would go under the tree. She was very much upset about Jed giving Bubba dog poop. She could not imagine him waking up on Christmas and getting nothing, while the other kids got something for Christmas. She did buy him a few things and hid them in the barn like Jed did with the mirror.

That night she wrapped presents and put them under the tree. Jed went out to the field and found some fresh dog poop. He filled up a bag and brought it back to the house with him. "Are we really going to do this to Bubba? I don't know if I want to go through with this," Virginia informed Jed. "We gotta do this or we will not be able to live with him before long. It's the best thing we could do," Jed explained. Virginia finally agreed, but that was only because she knew she had him some things in the barn.

Jed placed two piles of dog crap under the tree and had Virginia write Bubba's name on some tags, since Jed never learned to spell much. Jed stuck the name tags into the dog poop, and then looked straight at Virginia. "You know that we are doing the right thing for our son. If he don't learn now, when he gets to school those teachers are gonna be mad at us," Jed explained.

The kids were up early. They had made their way to the tree. Virginia was right behind them. She was handing out presents to each of them, except Bubba. When the last present was handed out, Bubba looked strange. He looked under the tree and saw the two piles of dog crap with the name tag sticking out.

Jed made his way to the tree. He could not wait to see the look on Bubba's face. "What's this name say?" Bubba asked Jed as he pointed to the name tag in the dog crap. Jed looked at the tag real close and said, "I think it says Bubba," Jed explained. Jed watched Bubba's face for a reaction. Bubba looked real peculiar then got up and started looking around the house.

Bubba went all through the house and then outside. He looked all around for something and then went back inside. "Well, what did you git for Christmas?" Jed said. Bubba turned and looked bewildered at Jed. "I thank I got a dog but I can't find the son-of-a-bitch anywhere!" Bubba exclaimed.

Jed and Virginia both were taken by surprise. They would have never suspected the answer. "Now look, Jed. The boy thinks he's got him a dog and it's your entire fault," Virginia informed Jed. Bubba continued to look around the house for the dog.

When Bubba was out of hearing range again Virginia said, "You will have to get him a dog now. You made him think he's got one," she told him. Jed just bowed his head. He knew that he lost again.

Virginia rushed out of the house and to the barn and fetched the presents that she had also got for bubba. She brought the presents back into the house and gave them to Bubba. "Santa had brought you some presents, but the dog your daddy got you pulled them out into the yard. Your daddy will look for the dog tomorrow and will find it for you," she told Bubba. He smiled and ran to Jed.

"Thank you, pa. What kind of dog did ya git me?" Bubba asked. Jed shrugged his shoulders and said, "It's just one of those that bark a lot," Jed replied. Jed never had or wanted a dog because he knew that they bark all of the time. He knew that his life was getting worse and Virginia was now taking them all to the dogs. Jed figured that Bubba would soon have the dog cussing too and making all kind of trouble.

Jed did just as Virginia had asked. He went the next day and found a dog that someone wanted to give away. He brought the first dog home and before he could get it in the door, the dog really did run away. Jed had to go all the way back to town just to find another dog. It was nothing but a mutt and Jed was right about the barking. It kept him up just about every night with the barking. Bubba took to the dog and it became a part of the family.

Somehow, dogs and wagons do not go too well together. Jed came home from work one day and saw

Bubba playing with the dog and the wagon. Bubba had the dog tied to the wagon and he was playing fireman with the dog. The dog would pull the wagon and made the most awful screaming sound that Jed had ever heard. Jed thought back in his recollection of dogs and he had never been aware that a dog could make such a sound. It did sound much like a siren on a fire truck. The noise would start out low and then scream louder until it reached a very high pitch. Jed was curious about the dog making the noise, so he went outside where Bubba was playing. That is when Jed noticed what was going on. Jed could not believe what Bubba had done.

Bubba had tied a rope to the dogs testicles and every time he wanted to hear the siren, Bubba would just tug real hard on the rope. Now Jed had a certain amount of compassion for animals and even had some for this creature that kept him up every night. He could not imagine what the poor animal must have been going through all day. He even thought about how it could have really been all week or month. Jed felt bad for the dog.

Jed stooped down beside the wagon and said to Bubba, "Why don't you tie the rope around the dog's body and have him pull you in the wagon?" Bubba had found him some chewing tobacco from the barn where Jed had him a stash. Bubba leaned his head over the side of the wagon and spit the tobacco juice on the ground. "Because if I do that, I will lose my siren," Bubba replied. The dog looked to the side and gave Jed a pitiful look. About that time Bubba pulled real hard again on the rope and the dog made the siren sound again.

Jed did deliver the dog from its captor and insisted that Bubba go and play with his train. Bubba was very upset that he lost his entire fire department in one day. Bubba went into the house and found his train that Virginia had gotten him for Christmas. He set the train up near the kitchen where Virginia was cooking dinner for the family.

Virginia had not been paying much attention to Bubba and his language since Christmas. She had forgotten that Bubba was still very much strong in the art of saying bad things. She had almost forgotten about it until this day came around. She would never forget it ever again.

Bubba loved the train set that Virginia had bought him. He played with it for hours at a time. It was non-stop fun for Bubba. He played like he was the conductor of the train and he was delivering people to and from the train station. He really used his imagination when he played, especially with the train set.

It wasn't until Bubba was in the middle of the game that Virginia finally noticed the language that her son was using with the train set. Each time the train would pass the play train station, she would hear Bubba say, "All those that want to get off, get the hell off. All of you that want to get on get the hell on." The words Bubba used slowly seeped around behind Virginia, and then ran straight into her ears. The words stung like a bee.

Virginia dropped the pot she had just filled with water and the water went everywhere. She raced into the room where Bubba was playing. "I have had enough of your dirty mouth, Bubba. Get to your room and think about what I told you about cussing," she told him. Bubba got up and stomped to his room. He was mad so he slammed the door behind him. Virginia was furious. "Wait until you pa gets home this evening. He will be mad too," Virginia said.

Three hours later Bubba peeked around the corner to see if his mother was in the room. She had went back to work in the kitchen so Bubba sneaked back to the train set. He was trying to be as quiet as he could possibly be.

He grabbed the controls of the train and around the track the train went. Bubba peeked around the corner to see if Virginia had heard the train. It looked like she had not, so he continued to play.

When the train got to the station, Bubba said in a real low voice, "All those who want to get off, get the hell off. All those who want to get on, get the hell on. All those who are pissed off about the three hour delay, talk to the bitch in the kitchen. She can give you your damn refund for being late".

Virginia stomped into where Bubba was at. She had heard everything that he had said. She grabbed up the track and train and went to putting the pieces into a box. "If that is how you are going to play, you are not going to get to keep what Santa brought you for Christmas," Virginia informed her son as she continued disassembling the train set. "Momma, you are gonna be responsible for all of those deaths if you keep on with that massive earth quake against the village," said Bubba. Virginia looked mad. She continued disassembling. "Earth Quake nothing. It's the end of the world for you and your train," she told Bubba. "All that want to get off, you'll have no choice but to jump to your damn death because Miss God is killing everybody today," Bubba said.

Virginia did not let Bubba play with the train again. She had made certain that if Bubba was not going to try and keep from cussing, he would not be rewarded. Bubba never did see that train set again and had wondered where his mother put the thing. He searched that farm from top to bottom, but never found one clue to where his train set had gone. Virginia knew that something was going to have to be done about Bubba.

When Jed came home from work Virginia informed him of the problem that she had encountered with Bubba and explained in detail what Bubba was saying. "I don't know what to do. Maybe they will know what to do when he gets in school," Jed explained. Virginia was not very excited about Jed's statement. She feared the day when she had to enroll Bubba into school. She knew that a whole new set of problems would begin and the old problem would not vanish from the horizon. "Jed, I don't think they will let Bubba stay in school," she informed her husband. Jed starred down at his hands. He was tired and really wanted to just sit down and relax without worrying about Bubba.

"We can cross that bridge when we get there," Jed said. Virginia looked sternly toward Jed. "We will be getting there much quicker than you think, and when we do you will be the one that will have to go to the school and figure out what disaster our son created," she informed Jed. He knew that Virginia was right and the problem did exist. He only hoped that the problem would come to an end on it's on, or that Bubba would just be more quiet about using his language. Jed knew that time had a way of changing things. He just wished the time would hurry and come.

Chapter Six

Bubba Goes to School

It was not until Bubba and his siblings reached the age of eight before they started to school. Other children wondered why Bubba and his brothers and sister were large children as apposed to the rest of the class. The teachers tried there best to make the transition for the Ledbetter kids a good one. They would tell the other kids that the reason those kids were so big was that they were eating all of their vegetables.

The Ledbetter kids took no prisoners when it came to bad luck and accidents. If you were near one of the

Ledbetter kids and an accident was going to happen, it was going to include you. That is why many of the kids learned quickly that hanging out with one of the Ledbetter kids could surely mean crying and pain. It did not take long for the other children to find out that piece of valuable information.

Now school and most of the Ledbetter kids did not mix very well. It would have been better to have sent them all to the army and hoped that the enemy was smart enough to surrender. The boys were all rambunctious, but to say that Betty Lou Ledbetter was an angel would be saying way too much. She had been the only girl in the family and being raised around three brothers was a fate that only a good tom boy could respect. She was not outright mean. She just had the tendencies of the Ledbetter family tradition of not using all of her intelligence at any given time.

A fine example of what I am talking about was on a fall day in Betty Lou's first grade class. The teacher had been to college and learned many things and special techniques to help him teach children. Betty Lou would change the way he saw things forever. The teacher was conducting a study in his class concerning children's senses. He was using a bowl of lifesaver candies to act as the variable in his experiment.

Now the teacher figured that giving the children all the same flavor of lifesaver would result in all of the children having the same answer. Betty Lou was the exception to the variable. The teacher handed out all the same flavor and asked the children, "What is the flavor, and what color is it?" The first color was red and all of the children, except Betty Lou said that it was cherry. Betty Lou was unsure. He passed out an orange-colored lifesaver to each of the children and asked the flavor, and what color it was? The children told him that it was orange. They were all positive of that and they felt that the flavor was also the same. They were proud of themselves for having the right answer.

Betty Lou still remained silent. She might not have been too sure about those answers, being that candy was not a big item around her house. The teacher was looking for some response out of Betty Lou so he figured that he would trick her with a flavor that was different from the standard lifesaver flavors. He passed out a honey flavored drop to the children and asked them the same question. He paid special attention to Betty Lou and hoped to get a good response. I don't think that he was ready for the response she gave back.

This time all of the children looked confused so he decided to give them a little hint and he said, "It's a flavor that your mother would call your father." All of the other children looked even more confused, but Betty Lou looked shocked and sickened. She slipped out of her desk and stood up. Suddenly, she spit the lifesaver out in the floor and made some of the most horrible gagging that you had ever heard. She shook and shivered all over. Before the teacher could say anything she had opened her mouth and shouted, "Everybody spit it out. They're assholes." The teacher stopped in his tracks.

Of course when you meet the Ledbetter family and they open their mouths, a new world begins to grow all around you. The teacher had opened Pandora's Box and there would be no way of ever closing it again. He would have been better off quitting that day and never returning to his job as a teacher at that school. Sometimes we learn the hard way and this teacher would learn new lessons each day that he would never ever forget.

On the first week of class, Leroy got into trouble for pulling a little girl's hair. He was sent to the office to report to the principal. He was waiting in the lobby to be called, when he overheard a conversation between one of the school maintenance men and the office clerk. Leroy immediately believed that he held the magic answer to the problem.

The woman clerk had hired the maintenance man to put some cow manure on her strawberries. Leroy misunderstood the conversation and approached the clerk and said, "Lady, you sure must be crazy or something. I don't know about you, but where I come from we put cream and sugar on our strawberries and we don't have to hire nobody. If you'll tell me where you live I'll throw some cow manure at your house for free." Nonetheless, the clerk was not happy with his reasoning and wrote him up again for bad manners.

A neighbor had been outside of the Ledbetter farm talking with Jed. After about thirty-minutes, Jed came into the house and was packing some clothes into a brown paper bag. Virginia noticed and questioned Jed about where he was going. Jed continued to pack the bag and he answered his wife. "I am gonna pack my clothes because I gotta go to the school about the kids again. I might as well just move in and stay at the school. I spend more time there than here," Jed explained. Virginia informed her husband that she would go to the school this time and give him a break. He agreed and quickly unpacked his paper bag.

Christmas time was approaching and Bubba was chosen to be one of the wise men. For what reason the teacher would choose Bubba, one could only wonder for the rest of their life. On the night of the play, the children were supposed to dress like the wise men and meet at the back of the stage. Bubba made it to the meeting place on time, but he did not seem to be dressed appropriately for the part of a wise man. The teacher was furious with Bubba.

"Why are you dressed like a fireman instead of a wise man? Did your parents not read my note that I sent home?" the teacher questioned. Bubba looked so serious at the teacher and said, "My momma was busy, so I gave the note to my daddy. He's got to where he can read pretty dang good," Bubba said.

The teacher was still mad. "Go get your daddy and tell him I want to have a few words with him about this," the teacher instructed Bubba and so he ran out into the audience to find Jed. After only a short time of looking,

Bubba had found his way to Jed. "Daddy, the teacher is mad at you something awful. She said it had something to do with the clothes that I am wearing. She said they don't match my part in the play and your reading stinks. You read her note wrong," Bubba explained.

Bubba knew that his dad was proud of his new found education of reading and he also knew that if he told Jed that the teacher thought he could not read, it would make Jed mad. Jed was furious by now. He was not about to let some teacher tell him that he could not read things right. Jed jumped up from his seat. "Where is she? I want to speak to her too. She is mistaken. I did exactly what the note told me to do!" Jed announced.

Bubba led Jed through the isle and to the back of the stage where the teacher was at. Jed walked straight up to the teacher and said, "Woman, you are wrong about me. I can read real good and I followed your note just like you asked." Jed informed the teacher. She looked at Jed with a smirk on her face. "You must be crazy, mister. Wise men do not dress like firemen."

Jed moved closer. "Yes they do," he said. "They do not," the teacher defended. Jed put his hand in his pocket and pulled out one of those pocket-sized bibles. "I guess that I'll just have to show you miss smarty," Jed said as he thumbed through the bible for the scripture that he was looking for. "I know the scripture is not in that Genius section at the first of the bible, but I will find it," he explained.

After only a few more moments, Jed had found the scripture that he had been looking for. "You see here. It says they came from afar. That tells me that the wise men were all far men," Jed explained like he knew the meaning of everything. The teacher just shook her head. She had no clue of how to win the argument. She felt defeated even though she knew she was correct. Bubba did not get to be one of the wise men that Christmas and Jed was mad for the rest of the year. He knew he was right and she was wrong and he or Virginia could not understand why Bubba was being picked on.

Back in those days the bible was taught at many of the schools. Leroy was a very good listener in class and many times he would take what the teacher said too seriously. For example, she could say that if you talk bad about people your nose will grow. Weeks after Leroy would hear something like that, he would pay more attention to his nose. If he said anything bad about someone, Virginia would have to spend hours convincing him that his nose was not growing. Vern started acting the same way and it wasn't long before Virginia had to spend most of her time explaining to her children that their body parts were fine and nothing was happening to them. Bubba was an exception. He never worried about something breaking off or growing the wrong way. However, he did have his own problems.

You remember back when I told you how Bubba would cuss all of the time? He never stopped. No matter what anyone would do he continued to cuss. One particular time that I remember is when he was working with his math at home. He was in his bedroom, doing his homework and reciting, "Two plus two, the son of a bitch is four; four plus four, the son of a bitch is eight; eight plus eight, the son of a bitch is sixteen."

Virginia was passing by his room and heard what he was saying. She was fit to be tied. She pushed open his door and walked straight up to him. "I thought I had made my self clear about your bad language. "You did, momma. The teacher told us to do this and say these things. I knew you would be mad if you heard what the teacher wanted me to say," Bubba explained.

Virginia was furious. She ran into the kitchen where Jed was sitting at the table. "That school is teaching our kids that cussing is fine!" she informed Jed. "You don't mean it?" Jed questioned. Virginia shook her head as if she did mean it.

"I guess you'll just have to go say something to the school about it," Jed told Virginia. The next day Virginia went to the school and confronted the teacher about telling her kids to cuss. She was not going to stand for that. She already had enough trouble out of Bubba without a teacher explaining that it would be fine for him to use bad language.

Virginia explained what had happened to the teacher. "I would like it if you didn't do that no more," Virginia told the teacher. "God Lord. That's not what I told them to say. They're supposed to say, 'Two plus two, the sum of which is four,'" the teacher explained.

Virginia was embarrassed for her mistake and apologized for the miscommunication. Of course that was just another day in the life of Bubba and how he saw the world. Virginia knew that she should have thought it out before she jumped and ran to the school. She knew that sometimes with Bubba, she should just wait.

However, she knew that trying to figure Bubba out was no less than trying to fly a rocket to the moon.

Now Betty Lou should have been the second child born. She had too many traits that were much like those of Bubba. The only difference is that Bubba seemed to get into far greater trouble than Betty Lou. Maybe it was the fact that she was smarter than Bubba, or it was the fact that people seemed to pay more attention to what Bubba was doing instead of what Betty Lou was doing. For example, Betty Lou came home from her first day of school and Virginia asked, "What did you learn today at school?" Betty Lou just shrugged her shoulders and said, "Must have not been enough. They want me to come back again tomorrow." That was just the way she saw things.

You see, Betty Lou would have been the most intelligent one of the two. She could say something that was dumb and not get into too much trouble. It might even have made sense if thought through. On the other hand, Bubba could say something and the world would come crashing down on his shoulders. Of course with Betty Lou, she may not have really meant the things she said. Bubba always meant exactly what he said.

Bubba did not make it through the third grade of school. By that time the school was willing to graduate him early and with honors if they had too. Bubba did not mind. He never liked school from the first day that he went. Within the first three months of first grade, Jed had to force Bubba to go back to school.

Bubba had a way about not understanding what people said to him. It was the third week of school and he was in class watching the teacher. The teacher had a lot to write on the chalk board and so she started reaching high atop the chalk board. Suddenly, there was a giggle from one of the boys in the class. She quickly turned and asked, "What's so funny, Mark?"

"Well, Ma'am. I just saw one of your garters," the little boy explained. The teacher became very upset at the boy. "Get out of my classroom. I don't want to see you for three days!" she informed the boy. He left the room and she started back to work.

The teacher realized that she had not put a title on her document at the top of the blackboard. She reached way up this time and started to write. Again she heard someone laugh out, this time the laughter was much louder.

She turned quickly to see this other boy. She was mad and he was going to get her wrath.

"What's so funny, Jerry?" the teacher asked. The boy was still smiling. "I saw both your garters and I thought they were funny," the boy explained. The teacher was ever angrier. "You get out of my classroom. This time I am going to make the punishment even more severe. I don't want to see you for three weeks," the teacher informed the boy. He packed his stuff and left the room in tears.

Now Bubba had been soaking all of this information in. He was new to information and he felt that he was getting the hang of knowing it. The teacher was very frustrated over the last two incidents in her class. She was nervous and she dropped her eraser on the floor. Without thinking, she bent over to pick up the eraser. Suddenly, she heard the strongest laughter of all and she turned around to see Bubba with his stuff and he was leaving the room.

"Where do you think you are going?" the teacher ask Bubba curiously. Bubba stopped and turned around to face the teacher. "You talking to me?" Bubba asked. The teacher said, "Yes, Bubba. Where do you think you are going?" she asked again. "Well, from what I just saw back there when you bent over, I figured my school days are over," Bubba explained. The teacher was totally confused and did not know how to handle the situation with Bubba. She knew that Bubba really believed that by him seeing what he saw, he believed that he was really done with school.

The biggest problem with Bubba is that he did believe everything he heard, thought, or said. That was also a problem for his father, Jed. I remember one of the neighbors wanted Jed to go hunting with him. He informed Jed that Bubba could come along too. They were walking in the woods and the neighbor said, "Look! A dead bird." Both Jed and Bubba looked up into the sky and said, "Where?" Of course the neighbor became frightened after he heard both their responses. He decided that it would not be a very wise idea if he were to be in the woods with Bubba and Jed and them with loaded shotguns.

Now Jed was real close to Bubba. It didn't matter that for several years Bubba had a close attachment to Betsy the cow. Jed had forgave Bubba for opening his eyes and seeing Betsy before he seen him. He just figured that was the time Bubba wanted to open his eyes and Jed figured that he was just not there at the special moment. Bubba did turn out to be Jed's closest son. Jed loved Bubba and spent many days teaching Bubba everything that he knew. Of course that was one of the problems to begin with. However, if Jed had not taught Bubba the first thing, Bubba would have still managed to get himself into more trouble than he would ever be able to remember in a lifetime.

Bubba always listened to his father and tried to do exactly what his father told him to do. The only problem with that situation was that most of the time Jed did not understand exactly what it was he was telling Bubba to do. For example, if Jed told Bubba to go get some hay out of the barn, Jed had to be very specific. If he was not, Bubba would end up bringing Jed all of the hay that was in the barn. That worked the same way for everything that was told to Bubba. If you told Bubba to feed the cow and did not tell him what to feed the cow, the cow could end up with big problems. That was Bubba.

Chapter Seven

Bubba and the Demons

A wonderful thing happens in each person's life at a certain age. They begin to grow up. Now for Bubba that was going to be a big problem. His life started to change and he got scared. As with all adolescent teen boys, their voices in most cases do not stay the same. Bubba's did not and he did not understand what was happening to him.

Now Bubba had been to church and he knew some things about god and he also knew some things about the devil. He had heard the preacher on many occasions explain how if you were bad, the devil was going to get you. He had also heard the preacher explain that if you were bad, god would get you too. Bubba felt that between the forces of good and evil engaged in war, somehow he had walked right into the middle of the battle and they were having a tug-of-war with his voice.

It was on a Sunday morning and Bubba had decided that it was time to go to church and try to make some kind of peace settlement between god and the devil. He had asked his mother if he could go with her to church on that day. She was surprised and actually thought that Bubba was about to turn over a new leaf. She welcomed him whole heartedly to join her in attending church. She had forced him many times to go to church with her when he was younger. Now he was growing up and she was proud that he decided on his own to attend the service with her.

When Bubba walked into church that morning you could have heard a pin drop. The congregation would not take their eyes off of Bubba. It was not that they were really surprised to see him. They just wondered if that was their day to die, or if the church was going to burn down first. Some may have even thought it to be a miracle from god, while others thought that the devil had sent Bubba to take them. Bubba did not care because he just wanted his voice fixed and he had heard the preacher talk before about miracles. Bubba sat down on one of the church pews to listen.

On this particular day, the preacher was preaching about how Jesus rebuked the demons out of this man and cast them into swine and the hogs ran into the river and drown themselves. Bubba was excited about this story. He knew that Jed had several pigs and he knew that all he needed was just one. He figured that it was a demon that was trying to take his voice.

Bubba sprang from the pew and yelled at the preacher, "Preacher, I'll be right back. I got a demon in my mouth and you can fix it for me," Bubba said as he left the church building. Virginia was not pleased and she worried about what Bubba had gotten into his mind. She knew that something was coming and she feared that what it was would surely embarrass her.

After only a short while Bubba returned and sure enough, he was carrying one of Jed's pigs. Bubba went straight up to the Alter of the church. "Preacher, I got this demon in my mouth and I want you to cast it out into this here pig," Bubba explained. The preacher could only guess that Bubba was talking about the cussing problem that he had, so the preacher told Bubba to come closer and he would try and cast the demon out.

Bubba moved as close to the preacher as he could and the preacher laid his hands on Bubba's head. Now that seemed to distress Bubba and Bubba said, "Preacher, the demon is not on top my head. It's in my mouth." The preacher looked deeply into the face of Bubba, something many feared to do, "Bubba, you have a cussing demon inside of you and I am going to cast it out into this here pig of yours. After I do I want you to take the pig down to the river and throw it in," the preacher explained. Bubba said, "If I do that Pa aint gonna like it none, but to get rid of this demon I guess I will." The preacher closed his eyes and had a peculiar look on his face, and then he said, "Demon, get out of this young man's mouth so he will not have a bad mouth anymore. Let this boy be in peace" Bubba said, "Yea, and get into this here pig of pa's so I can drown your ass, you son-of-a-bitch."

There it was. Virginia knew that something was coming that would embarrass her at her very own church and Bubba had delivered, just as she knew he would.

However, the preacher had an idea that he thought would help. He figured that if Bubba thought that the demon was gone, he might just stop using the bad language. The preacher continued to pray for Bubba and without letting Bubba see him; the preacher pulled a safety pin out of his jacket pocket. Suddenly, the preacher pricked the pig with the pin and the pig made an awful squealing noise. The preacher informed Bubba, "If you go now and throw this pig into the river, you will be cured. Go now, Bubba!" the preacher shouted. Bubba grabbed the pig and ran out.

Bubba ran as fast as he could with the pig. He held the pig at arms reach away from his body and especially away from his mouth. He felt that the pig had the demon inside. The pig started making strange noises and Bubba was spooked. Bubba had not noticed that the pig had just stuffed itself before he took it from the farm and all of the running and jostling was making the pig sick. It started to throw up all over the place. Bubba turned backwards and ran so the vomit could not get on him. He reached the river and threw the pig in.

Bubba returned to the church and the preacher asked him, "Did you throw the pig into the river as I asked?"

Bubba shook his head. "Sure did and I think the demon was trying to come back out of the pigs mouth. That pig spit demons at me all the way to the river and when I threw him in, I think I heard him call me something," explained Bubba. The preacher was curious. "What did he call you, Bubba?" the preacher questioned carefully. Everyone held their breath for the answer. "He called me a son-of-a-ham sandwich," Bubba explained. Virginia was surprised that Bubba had found a different word to use. "Very good, Bubba," the preacher said.

Now fate also had a great bearing on this day. It seems that Jed had decided to take a day off from the farm and go fishing. However, Jed was not having a good time. He kept arguing with this guy that was on the other side of the river. It seems that the guy was trying to get Jed to tell him how to get on the side of the river where Jed was. Jed said, "You're on the other side of the river." The man never could get Jed to understand what he wanted and finally gave up.

Jed had not caught anything all day and he had read in the bible that if you don't catch anything you are supposed to cast your line on the other side. He decided that he would give that a try before he called it a day. Jed drew back and cast the line hard to the side that he had not been casting on. "I don't care what size it is. If I catch anything we gonna eat it for supper tonight." Just as Jed was pulling the line in it caught onto the pig that Bubba had thrown into the water. Jed thought he had a whopper of a fish coming in. "This must be a whale," Jed said as he continued to real in his catch.

Just as the pig had been reeled into the sight of Jed, he became confused. "God works in some dang mysterious ways. I guess he created this here fish to look just like my favorite meat. He gonna be eat tonight," Jed said as he finished reeling in the pig. Jed carried the pig to the house and prepared it for the evening meal. Virginia had made it back to the house with Bubba. Bubba was proud that he had been cured of two problems. He felt that he no longer had a cussing problem and his voice should start stabilizing pretty soon.

The rest of the day was uneventful and Virginia began to prepare the evening meal. Jed handed her some wrapped packages and told her to prepare the meat that god had given them to eat for the night. She prepared everything and was thinking about how well the day had gone with Bubba getting cured of his problem. She had meant to mention to Jed what had happened to Bubba, but Jed seemed awfully busy. She did not want to disturb what he was doing, so she kept quiet.

Supper was finally ready and Virginia set the table. She called for Jed and the kids to come and eat. Meals at the Ledbetter house went quickly. If you were not at the table, you could miss something important. The family gathered around the table and Jed decided that since it was Sunday, and he was thankful that god sent him a fish that looked like a pig, he should say the blessing.

"Thank you, lord for this meal and this special fish that you sent to us," Jed said, then started to dip him a large portion of the different foods on his plate. All of the other kids followed Jed's plan and before long, they were all eating. Bubba was curious about the special fish that god had sent. "Pa, tell us about your special fish," Bubba said. Jed was always proud to tell about important things that happened to him, even if they didn't make any sense to the rest of the world. Jed put his special face on that he would have whenever he was going to tell a big story about something.

Now Bubba was asking for more than he had bargained for when he asked about the special fish. "Ok,

Bubba. I will tell you all about it. I was down at the river a fishing and hadn't caught anything all day. Suddenly, god made this fish turn into my favorite type of meat, "Pa, what is your favorite meat?" Bubba butted in. "Pork," Jed answered. Bubba looked real strange at his father who was sitting across the table from Bubba. "Did you say pork?" Bubba asked again. Jed shook his head in agreement. "Yes son. Pork is my favorite meat and god went and turned that big fish into a pig for me to eat tonight," Jed explained. Bubba thought for long time about what Jed had told him. He looked as if something was suddenly disturbing him. He turned to his pa and said, "That's awfully funny. I threw a pig into the river today and you caught a fish that looks like a pig," Bubba reasoned.

Jed stopped eating his dinner. "Why did you throw a pig in the river?" Jed asked Bubba. "Because that thang was full of my demons," Bubba replied. "Oh," Jed said as he continued eating. Virginia had already become too suspicious of what had happened. She had put two and two together and figured out that the pig Bubba threw into the river was the same miraculous pig fish that Jed reeled in. Nonetheless, Bubba would not let it go.

Something bad was flowing through his mind. "Pa, are you sure that this meat is a fish?" Bubba asked. Jed looked up at Bubba. Jed leaned on his elbows that were propped on the table. "I told you I caught him in the river, didn't I?" Jed responded. "Yes Pa, but tell me how you are so sure it was a fish. I mean, you don't think it could have been something else?" Bubba questioned.

By this time Jed had begun to wonder if he was being questioned about his blessing and it was making him mad. "Son, I am sure that this meat is fish. Just eat it and hush," Jed said. "But Pa, I think this could be the pig that I threw into the water and if it is, you gonna be cussing real soon and so am I," Bubba explained. Jed starred straight at his son. "I'll tell you how it went. I cast my line over to the side that the big fish was on and it took hold of the line. Now pigs can't swim and this fish was a swimming. He was swimming under the water and I know that pigs can't hold their breath that long," Jed explained.

Bubba was really concerned with the meat he had been eating. He was almost positive that it was the pig that he cast into the river. "What time did you catch the big fish?" Bubba asked. "Two o' clock," Jed said. "Well I cast the pig into the river at a quarter to two, so that means that the meat we eating now is that pig and now Ima gonna be repossessed by that stupid demon that was in the pig. I guess that means that Ima gonna have to go back to see the preacher next Sunday," Bubba said.

Virginia started to say something, but she stopped. She realized that maybe things were working out in the right direction. She figured if Bubba believed that he was repossessed that he would go with her to church again. She kept silent and continued her meal.

Vern reached across the table and thumped Bubba on his head. "Bubba, you sure are stupid. Pork chops don't come from a pig, they come from a fish," Vern said. "I know that, Vern, but this might not be pork chops we eating. This could be some pig," Bubba explained to his brother.

After dinner, Virginia explained the situation to Jed and informed him that Bubba would stop using bad language if he believed that the demons were cast into a pig. Jed agreed to allow Bubba to take one of the Pigs with him to church on the next Sunday. Bubba did and the preacher did his work, once again on Bubba. After that day, Bubba did get better.

Every so often, Bubba would let a small bad word slip, but each time he did he would return to the preacher for help.

There were plenty of flies around the church and the preacher finally informed Bubba that he no longer needed a pig to cast the demon into. He could use one of the flies that hung around the church to pester everyone. Bubba was curious about the fly thing. One day Bubba caught one of those flies that the preacher cast the demon into. Bubba decided he was going to bring the fly home with him to see if the fly would start cussing. He watched that fly for days, until Virginia finally informed Bubba that he would not be able to understand fly talk. Bubba just said, "Oh" and then drowned the fly. Bubba figured he was cured of the demons, because his voice had stabilized. He figured his voice had somehow been damaged by the demons because his voice was much deeper now.

Chapter Eight

Bubba Learns to Drive

Now Bubba had reached the age of seventeen and wanted to get a job away from the farm. Jed knew how Bubba felt and did not want him to be tied to working on a farm. Jed wanted Bubba to get him a good job and he wanted Vern and Leroy to also have them a job away from the farm. Jed had remembered how things were at that age on the farm. He remembered that was the same age that he had to get married. He figured that his boys should be able to get out and find them a much better job than he ever had. The biggest problem would be getting to the job. Jed knew that they only had the one mule and he needed that mule so he could go to work each day marking the trees for his father-in-law's logging company.

Jed knew that one of the boys would have to learn how to drive a vehicle. Jed and Virginia had saved a few bucks back and felt it was time to purchase a vehicle. Jed arose early one morning and had an idea. This would be the day that he would take his boys to town and buy an automobile. Jed was proud of his new found idea and felt that he had made the right choice. He awakened Bubba and Leroy and informed them of what his intentions were for the day. Bubba had been the one that Jed had chosen to learn to drive first.

"Who's gonna teach me how to drive when we get that new vehicle?" Bubba questioned. Jed put his old straw cowboy hat on and headed for the door. "Ima gonna teach you," Jed said. "Pa, I didn't know that you knew how to drive an automobile," Bubba said. "I didn't either," Leroy chimed in. Jed turned and looked at his boys. "Well I do know how to drive and Ima gonna teach you today," Jed explained as he ushered his boys outside.

Now Virginia knew better, but she remained quiet. She felt that today was going to be just another one of those disaster days that was waiting to happen to Jed. She felt that he and the boys would return home and the people from the town would be right behind them with pitch forks or something. She had no idea how exactly the situation would play out, but she knew that disaster awaited the end of the day.

Jed knew nothing about automobiles, but he had intentions of getting some old truck that the boys could lean how to drive. On this day Jed had decided that all three could ride on the mule to town. That old mule had gotten so old that it could hardly walk. It was a pitiful sight to see the three grown men on the back of the mule as it rode them toward the town. It could hardly walk and breathing was also a problem for the mule. Town was normally about an hour and a half ride for Jed on the mule. On this day it took four hours and that was with the boys pushing the old mule half of the way.

Jed had noticed a place that sold cars on the other side of town and they had made their way to the place. Paul Wright was the salesman and he noticed Jed coming toward the office. He was aware of the Ledbetter family and had no idea what they wanted with him. He met Jed about half way. "What can I do for you today?" Paul asked Jed. Jed pulled his old hat off and said, "Me and the boys are looking for us one of those vehicles that you have for sale". "What kind are you looking for?" Paul questioned. Jed looked strange and said, "One of those that you drive".

Of course Paul had never had a conversation with Jed and he knew that something was not right with Jed. He figured the least he could say to Jed the better. "Just tell me this; what kind of money do you have to spend on a vehicle?" Paul asked. Jed cocked his head to the side and said, "Well I had planned to pay for it with paper money, unless you want to trade for some hogs or produce". Paul wrinkled his eyebrow. "No, I mean how much money were you planning on spending for a vehicle?" Paul said. "Well I have about three hundred of those dollars that I can spend," said Jed.

Paul knew that was a very low amount to be spending on a vehicle, but he was a man that liked to help others. He knew that the Ledbetter family was poor and he felt maybe he should do his civic deed and help them get a vehicle. "I'll tell you what, I have an old truck out back and it is a good one. It is not that pretty or anything, but I think that it would work for you," Paul explained. Jed's eyes got really big. "Now it don't have to do much work for me, but the boys could use it to go to work with. How much you want for it?" Jed asked. "I'll take your three-hundred dollars that you said you have," Paul said. "Well let me see it," Jed said and Paul led Jed to the back of the office to show him the truck.

The truck was an old beat up looking truck, but when Paul turned the switch the truck fired right up. Jed walked all around the truck, looking for something that he did not know what. "What am I supposed to do to tell if I want this truck?" Jed asked. Paul looked confused and said. "I don't know. Just look it over and say if you want it or not". Jed looked all around that truck, and then said, "I want it or not". "No, you don't understand. I mean let me know if you do want the truck," Paul explained. "Oh, I thank that I do want the truck," Jed said.

Paul led Jed into his office to do the paperwork on the old truck. That was normally a quick process, but Jed didn't even know his own address and many of the items on the paperwork had to be left blank. Paul finished the best he could and Jed handed him a roll of cash. Jed could not count and he did not want his boys to do it for him, so he told Paul, "Just takes what's yours and gives me back the rest". Paul took his three-hundred dollars and handed Jed the rest of the money.

Paul led Jed back to the truck, where the boys were waiting. He handed Jed the keys and said, "It's all yours. Drive safely". Jed took the keys and thanked Paul for what he had done. The big problem was on the rise as none of them knew how to drive at all. "What we gonna do with the mule?" Leroy asked Jed. That was one thing that Jed had not counted on in his thinking. Jed thought for a long while, and then said, "We'll just put him on the back of the truck and let him ride that way home".

It took Jed, Leroy, and Bubba to get the old mule on the back of the truck. After that task was over, Bubba and Leroy crawled into the truck and Jed sit down on the driver's side. "Ok, Paw. Show us how to drive," Bubba said. Jed looked down to see if he could see what hole Paul had stuck the key into that made the truck start. Of course Bubba and Leroy were sure that their daddy knew about driving and all, but they were getting a little curious about if Jed knew where to put the key.

"It goes in that hole right there. I seen that man put it right there," said Leroy. Jed looked across at his son. "Don't you thank I know where it goes? I've a been driving these things since before you were born," Jed said. "Pa, where did you learn how to drive?" Bubba questioned. "There was this thank that came to town people called a fair. They had some cars in the room and you were supposed to git in them and not be hit by the other cars. I learned how to not be hit real well," Jed explained. The boys smiled because they were proud of their daddy.

Telling one thing and doing another can mean the difference between living and dying. The boys learned that lesson pretty quick after Jed had finally got the key into the switch and tried to start the truck. The truck had a straight shift transmission and Jed was not aware about the clutch. When he turned the motor over in the truck, that old truck leaped forward like a cat after a mouse. The old mule nearly went through the tail gate of the truck. Jed turned the switch back to off as fast as he could.

Paul had noticed the commotion and came out to the truck. "What's the matter, Jed?" Paul asked. Jed looked out the window at Paul. "I think something's wrong with the truck. It won't start like you made it and every time I try the truck tries to kill us," Jed explained. Paul knew the problem. Jed was not using the clutch or the brake. "Jed, here's what you got to do with this truck. You see that peddle on the left down below your feet?" Paul questioned. Jed looked down. He was not aware of what was left and what was right, but he did not want his boys to know.

"Yes sir, I see it," Jed said. "The first thing you gotta do is take your foot and mash it in before you try to start the truck," Paul explained. Jed took his foot and mashed hard on the brake peddle. "No Jed, I mean the other peddle," Paul informed Jed. Jed took his foot and mashed down on the other peddle, and then turned the key. The truck fired right up and this time did not jump across the parking lot. "I see. Now I remember, "Jed said. Paul knew that Jed had no clue of how to drive the truck.

"Why don't I get this man I know to show you how to work the truck," Paul told Jed. Jed looked at his boys to see if they were watching him. They had been looking out the other window and trying to take their hands and raise the window like it was one in the house. "Just tell me what I gotta do to make this thing move forward," Jed whispered. Paul finally realized that Jed had not wanted his boys to know that he knew nothing about driving a vehicle. Paul was a good man and he knew that Jed had very little pride. He knew that the small amount of pride Jed had he should get to keep.

"Jed, I think you could get killed with this truck if you are not careful, but I also think that there would be nothing I could say to stop you from driving this truck home. I guess with that, I better help you the best I can to know something about this truck. Just turn it off and follow me back to the office and I will do my best," Paul explained to Jed. There was a long silence between the two men and Jed reached down and turned the motor off.

Jed opened the door and informed the boys to stay in the truck until he returned. Jed walked with Paul to the office. It seemed like hours had passed before Jed returned to the truck and stepped back in. He put the key back in the switch, pressed the clutch down and fired the truck off. He remembered that Paul told him to let the clutch out slowly and the truck would move forward. He slowly started letting the clutch out, but not as slow as Paul told him to do. The truck leaped forward as it had earlier and stalled.

Jed fired the truck up again and this time he let the clutch out even slower. The truck began to move forward. Now this action seemed to please Bubba and Leroy as they were all excited. Jed managed to get the truck out into the road. He swerved left and right, but he managed to hold it in the center of the road. Suddenly a car was coming toward them from the front. Jed did not know what to do so he turned the switch off, causing the truck to stop in the middle of the road. The driver of the other vehicle was confused and he also stopped.

"Get out of the road!" the man in the car shouted. Jed looked angry. "We were here first. You get out of the road!" Jed screamed back. Paul was watching the commotion and he just shook his head in disbelief of how his day had gone. A train could have jumped he tracks from three miles down the road and ran through the side of the office and Paul would have thought no more of the situation.

Jed finally started the truck back and was slowly moving down the road again and passed the man in the car. Another big problem with Jed driving was that he had never really been aware of what the signal lights mean. He had walked across many of the streets in town and people would nearly run over him. He had never followed the directions for the lights and thought they were only there to make the city look good. Now Jed was driving a truck through town and he just ran all of the lights that were red.

Somehow the old mule seemed to be hanging on in the back of the truck. Jed was almost out of town, when he ran the last red light. The police chief had been parked on one of the roads beside the light. He was amazed at what he saw pass him. Jed was driving with Bubba and Leroy laughing and hanging out of the window. The old mule had hunkered down and all you could see was his butt sticking up out of the back of the truck. The chief did not feel like another incident with Jed and he decided against chasing after Jed.

Jed had driven out of town for about two miles, when he remembered that Paul told him something about that gear shift thing that was in the floor. Jed looked real close at the stick and decided that would be something he could learn on a different day.

Jed knew that too much education is a single day was not good for anybody. He felt that the education needed to go to Bubba.

If Bubba was going to learn to drive like him, he would need to start now.

Now Jed had not remembered the brake thing either. He had figured him a plan to which he could turn the motor off and the truck would eventually stop. He turned the motor off and sure enough, the truck slowly came to a stop in the middle of the road, just as it had done earlier when Jed was meeting that car. Jed stepped out and went around the truck to the other side. "Bubba, slide over into the driver spot and drive us home," Jed told Bubba. Now Bubba was more excited about what he was about to do than anything else in his life. He scooted over and Jed got in on the passenger side.

"Bubba, you been a watching me drive us?" Jed asked. Bubba looked over at Jed. "Yep, sure have, pa. I think I can do the same thing," Bubba said. Bubba turned the key on without pressing down on the clutch and the truck as usual leaped harshly forward, and then stopped. "See pa, I can do exactly what you showed me," Bubba said.

Jed was pleased with Bubba's actions, but he did not want Bubba to do the exact thing that he had done. "Bubba, just use that clutch thing and take us home," Jed said. Bubba shook his head and turned the key back on, this time with the clutch mashed in. The old truck fired right off and Bubba slowly let the clutch out. The truck moved forward and Bubba held it in the road. The only problem with Bubba was that he would keep giving the truck gas and letting off too quickly. The old mule kept sliding to the front, and then it would slide all the way to the back of the truck.

By the time Bubba pulled the old truck into their yard, both Jed and Leroy were pretty sick from the jostling. Bubba turned the motor off and stepped out of the truck. Virginia had heard the sound of the truck come into the yard and she stepped outside on the porch. She noticed her husband and Leroy were out on the ground and they were throwing up. "What's wrong with them?" she asked Bubba as he made his way to the porch. "They just can't handle the ride. Pa seen that Ima better driver than he is and it made him sick," Bubba said.

Virginia had remembered that all three had gone to town on Bubba the mule and Virginia was not noticing him on the back of the truck. "Where's our mule?" she asked Bubba. "That mule's on the back of the....," Bubba was saying as he looked toward the truck and noticed the mule was not there. "He was there earlier,"

Bubba said. By that time Jed had made his way to the truck and was looking in the back. "We lost him, Bubba," Jed said.

Bubba walked to the back of the truck and said, "Well he can't be lost. He's a hiding," Bubba said. Jed shook his head in disagreement. "He's not here, Bubba. We had to lost him on the road," Jed said.

"Pa, they taught me in school that if something don't fit, then something is wrong. See that gate thing on the back of the truck that opens and closes," Bubba said as he pointed to the tailgate of the truck. Jed looked at what Bubba was pointing at. "I see it, Bubba," Jed said. "If that gate thing is still closed, then the mule must still be in the truck. We call that deduction," Bubba explained.

Jed looked at the gate and said, "Bubba, I don't care what you call it at school. I call it gone and we gonna have to go get that old mule before somebody else finds him finders keeper and losers weepers. I don't want to be a weeping tonight," Jed informed his son.

Just as Jed was about to get back into the truck, the old mule came wobbling down the road. He was scratched and banged up, but he was still walking his way toward home.

It seems that the old mule like Jed's driving much better. When Bubba got under the wheel and was being slung around all over the place, the old mule decided right then that he might come out better if he just jumped from the moving truck. He knew that it was about his supper time and he wanted to live and get some of those oats he was fed everyday. He would rather have been a crippled mule eating oats, then a dead mule eating daisies.

The day ended without much damage to the town, the mule, or the Ledbetter family. Jed had learned partially how to drive and Bubba had learned the rest. Trips to town would be much better and the old mule felt that now he could retire and sit home eating his oats. That is how Bubba learned to drive.

Bubba Goes to Work

Bubba had been the only boy to learn how to drive, or shall I say partially learned to drive. Bubba could get the truck out on the road and make it go. He never found out how to make the truck go in reverse like all the other vehicles did. He just thought that it was some defect with the truck. He also never learned about changing the gears on the old truck and he drove it around in first.

Most of the people in town knew that when they seen Bubba coming, those traffic lights meant nothing. They would fair better by just letting Bubba get through the light before they tried to go.

Vern and Leroy were too afraid to get under the wheel of the truck and try to make it move forward. They felt that they should leave the driving to someone who had more knowledge of things and that person would be Bubba. The day came when the boys decided it was time to try and find a job. They looked everywhere for a job and finally a man needed some boys that could hand dig septic tanks for him. He hired the Ledbetter boys and they were to come to work the next day.

The boys returned home and informed Virginia and Jed about their new jobs. "We gonna be a digging some holes in the ground for this man. He said that the holes were to put these tanks in that hold people's crap," Bubba explained. "Yea, we gonna be some hole crapper diggers," Vern said. Jed and Virginia were pleased. It was the first job for their kids and they felt like proud parents.

Now the only one out of the Ledbetter family that did finish high school was Betty Lou and the school had actually let her pass so she would not come back. However, she had heard the boys talking and she was jealous. "How come they didn't finish school and they are the ones that get the job?" Betty Lou asked. Virginia tried to console her daughter. "Betty Lou, you know you need to go to college. I thought we all decided that you would be the one to go to college?" Virginia said. Betty Lou looked disappointed. "We did, but they still get to have all the fun," she explained to her mother.

The Ledbetter boys had no concept of business or management. They only knew that Jed was their boss and had never had a boss other than Jed. On the first day of work Virginia was up early and she was fixing lunches for her three boys. She had fixed their favorites, which was bologna sandwiches. She made certain that each one had plenty to eat. Jed had also got out of bed early as he would be taking on the duties of the three boys during the morning and they would take on the rest of their chores in the evening when they returned to work.

Jed shook their hands and told them that today they become men. Bubba said, "I know pa, and tomorrow we will git up and be men all over again". Virginia gave the boys their lunch and they left for work. Jed and Virginia watched as the old truck rolled slowly in first gear down the road and out of sight. "Our boys have finally growed up." Jed said. Virginia almost shed a tear at the thought.

The boys were not familiarized with how time worked when you were going to work and they were running late for the first day at the job. They finally rolled into the yard of the place they were supposed to work. The owner was digging a new septic tank for a couple that had changed their outhouse to inside plumbing. The boss had marked off the site for the tank to be built. He gave each of the boys a shovel and told them how deep of a hole he wanted dug.

Now the boss's job was only to watch the boys and make certain they did exactly what they were supposed to do. Bubba was not familiarized with this type of working conditions. It was in the hot summer and the humidity had grown very high on this day. Bubba, Leroy, and Vern had dug down about four-feet and the hole was beginning to look like a hole. Bubba was confused at why it was they were working so hard to get the job done, but the boss was sitting in the yard under a cool shade. He became frustrated and kept glancing at the boss. He felt like they were being used and the boss were just relaxing while they worked very hard.

Of course that was what a boss was supposed to do. Bubba turned to Vern and said, "What are we doing down in this hole doing the digging and the boss is up yonder under the shade tree a keeping cool?" Vern stopped digging for a minute and looked out of the hole at the boss. Vern said, "I don't know. I'll get out of the hole and ask him," Vern said. Vern laid his shovel down and climbed up out of the hole.

Vern walked over to the boss and noticed that the boss had him a nice cold soda pop and was sucking down the drink. "You boys thirsty?" the boss asked. Vern looked real close at the drink. "We might be a little," Vern said. The boss reached down into a cooler and pulled out three ice cold drinks. He handed Vern the drinks and Vern continued to stand under the tree.

"Is there something else that you needed?" the boss questioned. Vern scratched his head and said, "Well Bubba was a wanting to know why it was that we were working so hard digging the hole and you were just sitting here in the shade?" The boss gave Vern a smile and then explained. "Intelligence," was the answer that he gave to Vern. Vern looked confused and said, "I don't understand. What is it that you mean?" Vern questioned.

The boss moved from where he had been sitting and stood up to face Vern. "Well Vern, let me show you how this intelligence thing works," the boss said as he moved closer. "I'll put my hand on this here tree and I want you to hit my hand with your fist as hard as you can," the boss explained. Vern was reluctant to hit his boss's hand. The boss reassured Vern that it would be fine because of intelligence.

Vern agreed that he would hit the boss's hand so he drew back and took a mighty swing at the boss's hand. The boss moved his hand from the tree at the same time as Vern made the swing.

Vern hit the tree hard with his fist and immediately clutched his fist in agony. The boss said, "Now that's intelligence." Vern took the three drinks under his arm and went back to the hole. He was still in pain from hitting the tree.

Vern crawled back down into the hole and gave Bubba and Leroy one of the drinks. Bubba was curious about what Vern had learned about the boss. "What did the boss say about him sitting in the shade?" Bubba asked. Vern was still holding his fist, but he looked real serious at Bubba. Vern took a big drink of the soda pop and turned to Bubba. "The boss said that we were down here because of intelligence," Vern replied.

Now Bubba was confused about the answer. "What's intelligence, Vern," Bubba asked. Vern felt like he knew something that Bubba did not for once. He was proud of his new knowledge and wanted to share that knowledge with Bubba. Vern placed his hand on his face and told Bubba, "Take your shovel and hit my hand as hard as you can."

Bubba did exactly as Vern had asked, but he never found out what intelligence was. Instead he spent the rest of the day at the hospital with the doctor putting thirteen stitches in Vern's face.

Of course the boss felt that the boys were too big of a liability for him and paid them for what they had done. They had lost their job on the very first day and Vern gained some stitches to boot. He had never had stitches before and they hurt.

That night at the dinner table, Vern asked his father, "Hey pa, did you ever know what intelligence was?" Bubba butted in and said, "Pa, don't answer or we gonna end up back at the hospital again tonight," Jed was confused at Bubba's action and told Vern, "I'm not sure what that thing is, but you can teach me about it at a later time when your brother is not so upset about something."

The very next day Bubba and his brothers were out looking for a job again. They had heard someone at school tell them that if they do something and don't succeed, just try and do it better the next time. Now that was words Bubba could live by. He didn't like to lose and he felt that if he were to follow the education all the way, he would come out winning.

Now times were tough for the Ledbetter boys. Finding that job proved to be a difficult task. They searched everywhere to find work, but were always told the same thing about not having good enough insurance to hire them. Nonetheless, that did not fully discourage the boys. They still kept looking for the perfect job. Bubba was sure they would find that job. Unfortunately, after about two weeks the boys were getting weary of the search.

During Bubba's first few days of driving, he realized that the truck ate something called gasoline. It kept running out of the stuff and the truck kept stalling out. After about the third time a man stopped with some gas and explained to Bubba about how the truck needed the stuff to make the truck move. He also explained that you had to buy the gas like you would feed for the mule. Bubba kept pestering the people at the feed meal about selling him some gas for his truck. Bubba finally learned about gas stations.

Bubba and the boys had just about exhausted another day, looking for a job. They pulled into a gas station to get some gas. That is when they noticed a man with a roll of money coming out of the station. Bubba approached him and said, "Do you know where we can find a job and make some money like you have?" The man stopped and started talking to Bubba. "I make this money without working," the man explained. Bubba was surprised. He had never heard of a job that you didn't have to work at, but still made a lot of money.

"Well mister, tell me if I can get hired on at that job," Bubba said. The man pointed down the road. "Son, about fifty miles up that road is a place they call a casino. In that casino there are machines that you put money into. If your machine does right, you can end up with a lot of money for just a few dollars," the man explained. Bubba listened contentedly, knowing that he and his brothers would have to check the casino place out.

Bubba thanked the man for his help and crawled back into the truck. The brothers were excited about what Bubba had learned from the rich man. "Bubba, tell us what he said," Leroy insisted. Bubba smiled at Leroy and said, "Brothers, we gonna be rich. That man told me how to get money and we don't even have to work for it." The boys were thrilled as Bubba explained about the casino place. They made plans to go the next day. They all still had money from the last job, because they never went to any places to spend money.

The next day the boys were up early and were ready to go to the casino. Virginia was curious about what plans the boys had on this day. She asked Bubba about those plans. He said, "We gonna go to this casino and get rich. You put a coin in a machine and you win all kinds of money."

Now Virginia was not very familiar with a casino either, but she wondered why there would be a job that you did not have to work. She did not question the boys any farther, but she still was uncertain about the plan.

Bubba and the boys traveled slowly the distance to the casino. It was a big place and the Ledbetter boys were excited. They entered the establishment and went to the cashier, just as the man at the station had explained. They cashed all of their money in for quarters and each went their own way to different machines. They all had plans of striking it rich at the casino, just like the man at the service station had.

It was not too long before Vern and Leroy had run out of money. It seems their luck had not been that swell. They made their way across the casino and found Bubba. He had several buckets of quarters and he was excited. "Hey Vern, I'm getting rich over here," Bubba informed his brother. Both Vern and Leroy were curious as to how Bubba was getting all the money.

"How you do that?" Leroy asked. Bubba smiled and strutted over to his brother. "You see, I started losing my money on those machines there on the floor. I found me this machine on the wall and every time I put a dollar bill in this machine, I get back four quarters. We gonna be rich before I leave this here casino today," Bubba explained. The brothers were just as excited as Bubba. Unfortunately, someone finally explained the situation about the change machine to Bubba and he was truly disappointed.

The boys returned home depressed. When they got to the supper table Virginia had noticed their despair. "You didn't do to well with that casino place, did you?" Virginia asked. The boys dropped their heads and said,

"No" "Well I have some good information for you. Your grandfather came by the house and I told him about how you were going to get rich at the casino. He told me that you were not and informed me that he could get you a job planting new trees," Virginia explained.

The boys suddenly became excited at the new found information their mother held. "Grandpa is going to get us a job!" Vern said and the other brothers all jumped around like they were on fire. They could not wait to see their grandfather the next day. The boys ate very quickly that night and went to bed so the next day would come sooner.

The next day they did go to see Grandpa Haney. He helped them get the job and they became good at planting the trees. One day Leroy was out sick with the flu and it only left Bubba and Vern to work. Now they had a routine for planting trees and that routine was unchangeable to them. They had been working for the most part of that day and had worked themselves to an area that was next to a service station.

A man was at the station and he was drinking a soda, watching the two boys work. He became confused at what he saw. It seems that Bubba would dig the hole and

Vern would come right behind him and cover the hole up. The man could not stand the mystery any longer. He had to know why it was that two men would dig holes and just cover the holes back up without doing anything else.

The stranger made his way to where the boys were. He stopped right in front of Bubba and Bubba noticed the man. "What can I do for you, sir?" Bubba questioned. The man hesitated for a moment and then asked Bubba, "Why are you two guys digging holes in the ground and then just covering the holes back up?" Bubba looked surprised. "We a working, mister," Bubba replied.

The man was still confused. "I still don't understand what you men are doing on your job," the stranger said. Vern jumped into the conversation. He seemed a little mad at the stranger. "Mister, there are normally three of us brothers here doing the job. Bubba digs a hole, Leroy puts a tree in the hole, and I cover the hole back up. It is just that simple," Vern said. The man still was obviously confused because he still needed to know more.

"Pardon me, but I'm still confused. You are not putting any trees in the holes that you dig. Your just digging the holes and filling them back up!" the man said. Bubba looked strange at the man and said, "Sir, we can't help it if our brother is sick. We still gotta work and if he aint doing his job, that don't mean that we can't do ours." The man finally understood, but he understood that the boys were fools or something.

Leroy finally got over the flu and went back to work. That was a good thing because the boss said that he likes to see trees planted in the holes. The brothers loved the job and planned on making a career out of planting the trees. The boss had never been sorry for hiring the boys. He knew that sometimes they make mistakes and some of the trees didn't get planted, but he knew that the boys worked hard and had been taught to work hard.

Jed and Virginia were happy that the boys had found steady work. Jed knew the boys worked hard and he tried to cover most of the chores for the boys. Jed had only wished that he could have been so smart when he was growing up. He felt that he would have liked a job planting trees for a living. However, he also was proud of his job marking the trees for his father-in-law.

Chapter Ten

Stalking Bubba

One would think that girls did their best to stay away from the Ledbetter boys. Under most circumstances that would be true. However, there was a girl from town that paid much attention to Bubba Ledbetter. Faylene Weathers had her eye on Bubba since the first day she saw him in school. It was love at first sight for her and she always loved the way Bubba would say certain words. Most of those words were not to be said in public. That was back before Bubba had those demons removed from his mouth.

She found out that he worked planting trees and everyday she would sneak down to where Bubba was planting the trees and she would hide behind a tree and watch him. It was her intentions that someday she would call him her man and he would call her his wife. She had her plan for that day and it was all laid out. She did not care about what all the town folks would say about Bubba. She figured that if the other girls went on believing what the town folk would say about Bubba that would make him easy prey for her.

Bubba didn't know what he would do with a girl if she did like him. He had some problems early in life when he was in school. One of the teachers was being nice to Bubba after she had seen one of the girls be rude to him. The teacher told Bubba that he was a good looking boy and that he should catch him one of those girls. Of course Bubba took what the teacher told him literally. Jed had taught all of the boys to trap animals when they were little. Bubba thought what the teacher had told him was one of those trappings.

Bubba made him a trap out of a rope and then waited until the time was right. He had his eye on this one girl that he thought was pretty and when the moment was right; the girl was hanging from her ankle in a tree. The teacher spent the next two hours explaining to the principal that Bubba didn't mean to do that. He had misunderstood what she had told him. The teacher assured the principal that she would not tell Bubba anything else that he could get wrong.

Now Faylene was a very pretty girl and she had always stayed at a distance from Bubba. She was afraid to speak to him when she was a young child. She feared that her parents would prohibit her from ever having anything to do with Bubba. Now that she was older, they would not be able to stop her if she did want to see Bubba. Her family was not very wealthy and they too were back wooded.

One day Faylene got tired of hiding in the background and decided that she should try and talk with Bubba. She had also been taught to trap when she was just a girl. She figured that she would make her a plan and just put Bubba in a predicament that he could not get out of. If things did not work out like she had planned, she could always tell him that it was just an accident.

She had watched and noticed that Bubba would sometimes go fishing at the river with Jed. She figured that she would let him do his fishing and would trap him on his way back home. Bubba usually would lag behind and fish just a little longer than Jed. Faylene was going to make the best of this day. Unfortunately, this was a day that Bubba decided to go to church.

She had set the trap and kept looking for Bubba. He was no where to be seen. Jed had made it down to the river and he was going to fish on this day. Faylene was making too much noise and Jed thought that Bubba or one of the other boys was there to pull some kind of trick on him. They had a habit of pulling tricks on Jed and Jed had decided that it wasn't going to happen on this day.

Jed had spied something in the thick part of the trees and he decided that he would jump in the river and slip around behind where the noise was coming from. He was going to scare the living daylights out of those boys. He made his way behind where the noise had come from and closed in on his prey.

Suddenly, he jumped and grabbed Faylene and tried to wrestle her to the ground. She kicked him in the groin and he fell to the ground in pain.

"Mr. Ledbetter, I never thought that was you," she informed Jed apologetically. He finally regained his composure and asked her what it was that she was doing in the woods. "Well I was trying to see your son, Bubba. I wanted to talk to him and I figured that the only way I could talk was if I trapped him," Faylene explained.

Jed assured her that he would have a talk with Bubba and see if he could get Bubba to talk with her. Faylene apologized again and was on her way home.

Now Jed was surprised that a pretty girl was after one of his sons. He had hoped that one of them would end up being the woman's man. He figured that would be Vern and not Bubba.

That evening Jed told Virginia all about what had happened. She was shocked. She could not believe that a girl was after her Bubba. "Jed, it's only been like yesterday that Bubba was in the floor paying with his toys," she told Jed. Jed looked at her strangely.

"What are you talking about, Virginia. Bubba still plays in the floor with his toys," Jed informed his wife. "I know, Jed. That is what I'm talking about," Virginia said.

Jed thought back to his recollection with love. He remembered everything. "Virginia, do you remember when I was seventeen and you asked me to go to the barn with you. I remember how when we got there you asked me if I would marry you," Jed informed his wife.

She looked at Jed like he had lost his mind. "You are stupid. I never asked you to go anywhere. It was you that caused us to have to get married over a stupid gun," she reminded Jed. He looked pale. He had forgotten all about the shotgun wedding. He remembered.

"What are we gonna do? If Bubba takes her into a barn he is through," Jed said. Virginia shook her head in agreement. "Maybe we can hide Bubba from this girl," Virginia said. Jed disagreed. "We can't do that. If we do he may never have a chance at love," Jed explained. "What if the girl is dumb?" Virginia questioned. "She likes our Bubba. She can't be that dumb," Jed said.

The two sat silent for a very long time and then Virginia broke the silence. "Jed, we cannot stand in front of happiness for Bubba. If this girl wants to see Bubba, we got to let him see her," Virginia explained.

Jed rubbed his forehead. He was worried. He turned to Virginia and said, "Maybe we can just lock up the barn and Bubba can't take the girl in there," Jed explained. Virginia agreed and they decided to tell Bubba about the girl that wanted to see him.

Bubba had been out back feeding the old dog that Jed had got for him when he was a boy. Jed called out and motioned for Bubba to come into the house. Bubba heard Jed and made his way to the house.

Bubba was in the kitchen and was looking for something to eat. He had started to eat some of the dog's scraps, but remembered how his grandma Haney explained he could get sick if he eats food that was left out.

Bubba always watched the old dog after he fed him to see if the dog died. Bubba did not comprehend the fact that animals could eat scraps that were left out and boys could not without getting sick. Bubba would watch the dog closely every time and the dog would be bothered by Bubba doing this. The old dog would try to go somewhere else to eat after Bubba would give him the food. Bubba would follow.

Jed and Virginia walked into the kitchen where Bubba was at. "We gotta talk to you about something, Bubba," Jed said. Bubba continued to sit and look dumb. "It looks like a girl wants to meet you and talk to you," Virginia explained. Bubba shrugged his shoulders and said, "About what?" Virginia moved in front of her son.

"She wants to talk to you about dating her. She wants to go out on a date with you," Virginia explained.

Now that piece of information took Bubba by total surprise. He had not planned on his parents telling him something like that. He didn't even know if it made sense to him. "What do you think she is wants to do on this here date that she is planning behind my back," Bubba said. Jed jumped right in the middle of the conversation and said, "She don't want to be going in no barn, that's for sure." Jed said. "Yes Bubba. No matter what happens stay away from the barn and you will be ok," Virginia said.

Bubba was too confused. He had not ever thought about how to go on a date and how to make a girl like him if he did go out on a date with her. He was not even sure what exactly a date was. He knew that he had better find out pretty dang quick. "Pa, what exactly is a date?" Bubba questioned. Jed looked at Virginia. Jed did not know exactly what a date was either. Virginia looked right back at Jed. She too was unsure about the answer.

Jed was getting nervous. He motioned for Virginia to follow him into their bedroom so he could clarify a few things. Bubba was going to follow and Jed said, "Bubba,

I got something in my eye and I want your mother to help me get it out. You stay here until we get back," Jed informed his son.

Virginia got up from the table and followed Jed into the bedroom. "What is a date?" Jed asked his wife. She shrugged her shoulders. "How could I answer that? I don't know if we ever been on one before," Virginia explained. Jed looked spooked. "You don't reckon she's a wanting to take our son to the barn, do you?" Jed questioned.

Virginia looked strange. "I don't know. If that was a date you carried me on to the barn, we never came back from it," Virginia informed her husband. "We can just keep our barn locked up while the girl is here," Jed said. Virginia agreed.

Jed and Virginia went back to the kitchen to talk with Bubba. "Bubba, a date is where you go somewhere and do something really scary," Jed explained. Virginia looked sharply at her husband. She did not want him to give away the secret to what had happened to them when they were young. "Bubba, what your pa is saying is that dating is something scary so you have to be careful," Virginia said. Bubba said, "Ok."

Jed met with Faylene at the river the next day. "Bubba said that he would go on this date with you, but remember that he don't like those barns and he will go with you only if you keep him away from barns," Jed said. Faylene agreed and the date was set for the following night. Bubba would pick her up at the bridge that crossed the river. It would be his first date and it would be on Halloween night.

Chapter Eleven

Dating Bubba

Halloween had come and Bubba was in a hurry to get out of the house before it closed down, due to the little creatures that lurked around on that night. The Ledbetter family had never gotten use to that night. Back when Virginia had lived at home with her parents, they lived so for back in the woods that the trick or treaters never came to their house. Jed also lived way out and he was never visited by the creatures on that night.

As the years past, things changed. Jed had opened the door to a knock on this one certain Halloween night. He passed out in the floor and when Virginia heard the fall, she rushed into the living room. Little small monsters were hovering around her husband chanting things like, "We want candy. Trick or treat". Virginia had no idea as to what the scary things were, but she took a broom and chased them out from the door. When Jed awoke he was scared almost to death. He had never seen creatures before and had never heard of them coming to peoples homes.

Bubba and his siblings hated that night too. It made them mad to think that Santa Clause would not stop by their house and would leave the presents at their grandparents, but the monsters would always come like clockwork. Jed had made a plan for everyone to stay in the back of the house and keep all the lights off. Jed said that the lights attracted the creatures to the house.

Now when Jed was making the dating plans with Faylene, he never mentioned a certain time that Bubba would be coming to pick her up. She had waited on the bridge for the most part of the day. Bubba had spoken with one of Jed's co-workers about the date situation and needed some information that might help impress the girl. Bubba came home loaded down with the information. It seems that all he needed to impress this girl was a thing they called an eight track tape player. Bubba had stopped by the store early in the day and bought one of those things.

Bubba was not the master of electrical mechanics and he had never worked on the truck. He spent most of the day trying to hook up the tape player so the Faylene girl would be impressed. He managed to get the thing out of the box and mount it on top of the dashboard of the truck. That is about as far as he got. He decided that he would come up with another way to impress the girl and make her think the tape player was working fine.

Bubba finally pulled the truck out of the drive and made his way up the road and to the bridge. The girl was sitting on the edge of the bridge and Bubba could see her from a distance. The closer he got to her, the prettier she was. He couldn't believe his eyes and he knew something was up. He came to a stop next to the girl. Bubba rolled down the window of the truck.

"Ima looking for this girl named Faylene something or the other. She's a wanting a date with me," Bubba said. Faylene smiled at Bubba and said, "I guess I would be that girl'. Bubba reached down onto his leg and pinched himself. He was not asleep and this was the girl that had been looking for him.

Bubba stepped out of the truck and closed the door. He looked Faylene up and down and said, "I reckon you might be pretty. What we gonna do?" Bubba asked. Faylene walked around Bubba and looked him up and down. "I reckon we going to go somewhere and have some fun. This is Halloween night and people have fun on this night," Faylene informed Bubba.

Bubba looked strange. He had not figured on this night being too fun with all the monsters that came out. He guessed that the girl knew something that he did not. He walked to the passenger side and opened the door. "Git in Faylene girl. I guess we can go and try to have some fun somewhere," Bubba told her. Faylene followed Bubba's instructions and got into the truck.

Bubba walked around to the driver's side and got into the truck. He just sat there. "I don't know where to go on this night and have some fun," he told Faylene. She smiled at him and said, "Just crank the truck and I will tell you where we can go. You'll be glad you did," she informed Bubba. Bubba started the truck and pulled forward. He was on his way to somewhere.

After only a moment, Faylene began to explain some of the rules to Bubba. "I know where this old cemetery is that folks like us go to and have fun," she explained. Bubba looked real weird at Faylene and said, "I don't know about that. I imagine those people at the cemetery don't have too much fun." Faylene started to laugh at what Bubba said.

Faylene noticed how serious Bubba looked because she was laughing. "Bubba, I really like you and I think everything that you say is funny," Faylene informed Bubba. He begun to relax and not take Faylene as serious. "The only thing about tonight is that you have to get me home by one o'clock in the morning. If you don't, we both gonna be in some real big trouble," Faylene said. That seemed to scare Bubba. "You reckon I need to take you on home?" Bubba said.

Faylene laughed again at Bubba and he figured that she was just joking. He did not know anything that he was supposed to do on that date. He remembered what one of Jed's co-workers had told him. Bubba acted as if he was sticking a tape into the tape player. He noticed that Faylene was watching his every move. He felt that she would not notice him if he did something.

Bubba turned his head away from Faylene and started humming a song real low. Faylene did notice and she asked him, "What song is that you are humming?" Bubba was surprised and said, "You a hearing the tape player. That's not me". Faylene smiled and said, "Well, the tape player sounds awfully good".

For the first time Bubba had taken notice of a girl and she fascinated him. She had all of the qualities that he would have liked in a girl and she seemed to like him. He felt that this was going to be a good night for him and a night that would change his life forever.

They drove for what seemed like an hour. Faylene had led Bubba up dirt roads that he had never seen before. Finally, Faylene informed Bubba that the old cemetery was just ahead on the right. Bubba pulled in and parked. There were no one else around and Bubba felt spooked of the situation.

"They aint anybody her, Faylene girl," Bubba said. Faylene turned around to face Bubba. "I know. We probably are going to be the only people up here tonight. This is where my grandmother is buried and I always did want to take you up here at night," she informed Bubba.

"Why we here?" Bubba asked. Faylene scooted closer to Bubba and said, "This old cemetery is haunted. They are ghost up here". Well that did not do any good for Bubba. He had enough of them at home on this same night and this date thing sounded a lot like the house.

Bubba turned to look at Faylene. He was about to tell her they were going to leave and go somewhere else, until he seen her shiny blue eyes. They were big and looked a lot like the moon to Bubba. He could not help but look deeply into them. They had him and he was under a spell.

"What you gonna do to me. You one of those there witches and you got me under some kind of a spell, aint you?" Bubba questioned. Faylene laughed at Bubba again. "I aint no witch and I aint gonna do nothing to you. I just want for us to be together and talk about all kinds of things," she informed Bubba. Bubba shook his head as if he agreed to do that for her.

She informed Bubba about how she had watched him while she was in school and how she had hoped to talk to him one day. Bubba was amazed that the pretty girl would have an interest in him. He had begun to think good things about the girl. She had touched his heart in a way that no one ever had. He really did not want to go. He really was having him a dang good time.

Bubba listened to everything that Faylene said to him. He paid a lot of attention to her eyes. There was just something about the girl's eyes that kept him interested in what it was that she had to say. Most of the time, Bubba was not interested in what a person's eyes looked like. There was just something about this Faylene girl and her eyes that he could not be attracted from.

Bubba began to tell her about his family and life and about his pa's sisters that he never met. He rattled on and on about all of the secret and private things that he had done in his life. Just like Bubba, Faylene was attracted to his eyes and she listened to everything that he had to say. Finally, Bubba stopped talking and Faylene asked him if he would like to see the inside of that old haunted church.

Bubba reluctantly agreed and opened the door to the truck. Faylene hurriedly got out and met Bubba in front of the truck. "You can't kill a ghost and I don't like something that is dead a trying to talk to me," Bubba informed Faylene. "Don't worry. Those ghosts have got to be friendly," Faylene said.

Bubba followed Faylene toward the church. "I aint heard of any friendly ghost," Bubba said as he followed. Faylene reached the door. There was a moon, but clouds had begun to cover and everything got darker. Faylene opened the door to the old church. "Hello," Faylene yelled into the church.

Now Bubba figured that being in an old cemetery at night was not the best idea for him and yelling into a church had to be on the top of the list of things not to do. He followed Faylene inside the church and they stopped and listened to the quietness of the church. There were no sounds at all and Bubba did not like the quietness. "I think it would be a good idea if we were to git away from this place," Bubba said.

Faylene looked at Bubba. The room was dark, but Bubba still noticed those big blue eyes. His attraction for Faylene was paralyzing much worse than the fear of the dead. Suddenly, a chilling sound of someone moaning came from inside the church. Faylene looked coldly at Bubba. "You hear that?" Bubba said. "I did and I don't know what it was. We are supposed to be alone," she informed Bubba. "Well, we aint alone and somebody's a moaning in that church," said Bubba.

Bubba took Faylene by the hand and pulled her back to the truck. He did not know but that was exactly what Faylene had wanted from the beginning. She had wanted him to hold her hand. After only a moment they were back inside the truck. Jed was locking the doors and his eyes met with Faylene's. He was instantly under the spell again. He could not move.

Faylene moved closer to Bubba and kissed him on his lips. "What was that," Bubba said. Faylene pulled a way and said, "That was a kiss that said something," Faylene replied. Bubba looked and felt strange. "Well what was it that it said?" Bubba asked. Faylene pulled Bubba close to her and said, "I love you, Bubba Ledbetter".

Now Bubba was in a state of shock. He had not ever heard another girl say anything like that to a boy. However, he was under her spell and she was the one that had all the magic. "What would you say to me?" she asked Bubba. He continued to look deeply into her eyes and said, "Being that I can't get out of this spell, I would say that I love you," Bubba said and kissed the girl.

Now time had slipped by and Bubba remembered what Faylene had told him earlier about her being home by one o'clock. That time was drawing near and he knew that he did not want to be in a lot of trouble. He pulled away from Faylene and said, "We gotta go or we gonna be in a lot of trouble." Faylene looked worried about something. "I got to get out and use the bathroom. You stay right there," Faylene informed Bubba.

She had nothing to worry about. Bubba had never seen a girl use the bathroom and didn't know if he ever wanted to. Faylene opened the door of the truck and got out. She made her way to the back of the truck. Bubba stayed in the truck and thought a lot about Faylene and tonight.

Now Faylene Weathers was up to something and Bubba was dumb to the entire thing. She had taken a knife from her father's hunting jacket and she had it with her. Faylene stooped down at one of the back tires of the truck. She opened the knife and stabbed it deeply into the tire. She moved away from the tire and returned to the inside of the truck with Bubba.

Bubba had heard something spewing and he had thought that Faylene had drank way too much of something because the spewing lasted a long time. Faylene pulled herself back into Bubba's arms. "You still love me?" she asked Bubba. Of course Bubba was still under her spell. It did not matter if she had been outside for a little time. Bubba was still hexed by the girl. He looked deeply into her eyes and said, "Yep, I thank me still do love you".

They kissed again for a long time. Bubba suddenly remembered the time and informed Faylene that it was time to go. They were already going to be late. Bubba fired up the truck and started to move down the road. Bubba had noticed that something strange was wrong with the truck. It did not drive the right way and was making all kind of noise.

Faylene looked at Bubba and said, "I think we have a flat tire". Bubba looked strange. He did not understand what she was saying. Faylene realized that Bubba had not understood her. "One of the tires on the truck that makes us go is not going right," Faylene said. "What do I do?" Bubba questioned. "The first thing you supposed to do is stop the truck," Faylene told Bubba.

Bubba pulled the truck to the side of the road and got out. He looked at all of the tires and noticed that one of them was flat. "My truck is broke. What am I supposed to do about that?" He said. Faylene had also got out of the truck and she too was looking at her handy work. "I guess you'll have to change the tire," she told him.

Bubba had never changed a tire before in his life. He had not realized that you were supposed to change them. "Reckon this happens a lot to people?" Bubba asked. Faylene smiled at Bubba and said, "It does. All you got to do is change the tire and put the spare tire on." Bubba looked bewildered. "What's a spare tire?" he asked.

Faylene walked around to the side of the truck where the spare tire was mounted. She unscrewed the bolt that was holding the tire in place and pulled the tire down. "Well, I'll be. I thought that was some kind of an ornament for the truck," Bubba said. Faylene laughed.

Faylene realized that since Bubba knew very little about what was going on, she would take advantage of the situation. By the time the tire was changed it was almost morning. Bubba was worried. "I guess that time limit could not have meant one o'clock this evening, could it?" Bubba questioned. Faylene said, "It was this morning and we in trouble". Bubba dropped his head. He knew that he was in some kind of trouble that he had never been in before in his life.

Jed and Virginia were worried that their son had not came in all night. Virginia had remembered her sister and how she had not come in all night. There was a wedding and everything after that incident. She just hoped her son was doing ok and had not been hurt by anything. Jed had packed the old mule with a saddle and he and Virginia were going to go out looking for the boy.

Bubba raced in first gear as fast as he could go to try and get Faylene home. They finally reached the driveway to her house and Bubba pulled in. "The house is on up the road," Faylene said. Bubba continued to drive up the road. He pulled in front of the house and turned the motor off.

Faylene reached over and kissed Bubba on his lips. "I do love you, Bubba Ledbetter," Faylene said. Bubba smiled and said, "I do love you too, Faylene girl." About that time someone had snatched the door of the truck open and was holding a shotgun on Bubba. "What you a doing?" Bubba questioned the man.

Now Bubba was not aware that the man was Aubrey Weathers, Faylene's father. "You two get out of that truck and I mean now!" Aubrey demanded. Bubba was surprised, but he got out of the truck. "Sir, there is a big misunderstanding about what is going on here. I know your daughter was supposed to be home early this morning, but the truck had a broken tire," Bubba said.

Jed and Virginia had made their way to town and the chief of police had informed them where Faylene Weathers lived. Jed drove the mule out to the house where Faylene lived. Just as they rode into the drive, they seen Aubrey with a shotgun pointed at Bubba. They could not believe their eyes. Bubba was in trouble.

"What's a going on here?" Jed asked. "Is this your son?" Aubrey Weathers asked Jed. Jed shook his head. "Yep, this is Bubba, my son," Jed explained. Aubrey looked angry at Jed. "Your son has been out all night with my daughter and I know they been a lovin or something," Aubrey said. Jed dropped his head.

Virginia could smell a rat. She knew her Bubba was dumb, but she also knew that he didn't know anything about loving. She called Faylene away from the truck and said, "What's going on here. You know Bubba didn't do anything wrong". Faylene dropped her eyes to the ground. "Don't say anything to stop this. I love him and I just want to be living with Bubba," Faylene explained.

Virginia took Faylene by the hand and was leading her toward Aubrey. "You going to tell your father just what happened and how you been hanging out around our house to try and snag Bubba!" Virginia demanded.

Faylene tried to hold back, but Virginia was strong and she continued to pull her forward. Jed was arguing pretty strongly with Aubrey about that time.

All of sudden, Bubba jumped up and said, "I really did do it. I did love on that girl and I guess I need to pay for what I have done". Virginia stopped dead in her tracks. Jed's mouth flew open and Aubrey dropped his head. Aubrey had really only wanted for Bubba to convince him that nothing had happened with his daughter. Now the truth was out and it would have to be dealt with.

Virginia slowly moved next to her son and asked, "Bubba, did you really do anything with this girl?" Bubba smiled at his mother. Virginia recognized the smile. It was one like Jed had given her when he first realized that he was madly in love with her. "I love her and she loves me. I got me a woman now," Bubba said. Aubrey had heard Bubba. "You got you a shotgun wedding, boy," Aubrey told Bubba.

Jed moved close to his wife and said, "Reckon we gonna have to tell these two about those birds and those bees?" Virginia smiled and kissed her husband. "We will have to do just that," she informed her husband as she hugged him tightly.